MEANING-*FULL* DISEASE

MEANING-*FULL* DISEASE

How personal experience and
meanings cause and
maintain physical illness

Brian Broom

KARNAC

First published in 2007 by
Karnac Books Ltd.
118 Finchley Road, London NW3 5HT

British Library Cataloguing in Publication Data

A C.I.P. for this book is available from the British Library

ISBN-10: 1-85575-463-0
ISBN-13: 978-1-85575-463-8

Typeset by Vikatan Publishing Solutions, Chennai, India

Printed in Great Britain by Biddles Ltd., King's Lynn, Norfolk

www.karnacbooks.com

CONTENTS

To Alison, again

ABOUT THE AUTHOR

Brian Broom is adjunct professor at the Auckland University of Technology, Auckland, New Zealand, and leads the post-graduate programme in MindBody Healthcare. His other book is *Somatic Illness and the Patient's Other Story. A Practical Integrative Mind/Body Approach to Disease for Doctors and Psychotherapists.* He works as consultant physician (allergy and clinical immunology), psychotherapist, and mindbody specialist, at the Arahura Health Centre, Christchurch, New Zealand.

ACKNOWLEDGEMENTS

The Editors of Advances in Mind/Body Medicine, a publication of InnoVision Health Media (www.innerdoorway.com), have kindly allowed me to re-use some clinical cases/stories from two of my previous articles as follows:

a) The case of Patient Z (p. 163 in Advances) called 'Eunice' in chapter 3, and the patient cameos (p. 167 in Advances) in chapter 7, originally described in Broom, B.C. (2000). *Medicine and story: A novel clinical panorama arising from a unitary mind/body approach to physical illness*. Advances in Mind/Body Medicine, 16: 161–207;

b) My own 'story' (p. 28 in Advances) in chapter 13, originally described in Broom, B.C. (2002). *Somatic metaphor: A clinical phenomenon pointing to a new model of disease, personhood, and physical reality*. Advances in Mind/Body Medicine, 18: 16–29.

Georg Groddeck's case (in permitted abridged form) of the shoemaker with retinal haemorrhage, used in chapter 1, is from *The Meaning of Illness. Selected Psychoanalytic Writings by Georg Groddeck*, published by The Hogarth Press and the Institute of Psychoanalysis. Reprinted by permission of The Random House Group Ltd. Also: By permission of Paterson Marsh Ltd on behalf of The Estate of Georg Groddeck.

Sincere thanks are owing to Zoltan Kovecses, Professor of Linguistics at Eotvos Lorand University, Budapest, who has generously permitted use of comments he made during a brief but stimulating cross-disciplinary e-mail conversation concerning 'somatic metaphors.'

The story of Patient T., briefly summarised, and discussed here in several chapters, was originally published in full *in* Broom, B.C. (1997). *Somatic Illness and the Patient's Other Story. A Practical Integrative Mind/Body Approach to Disease for Doctors and Psychotherapists.* London: Free Association Books. The theoretical issues discussed in respect of this case are published here for the first time.

PREFACE

Meaning-*full* diseases have the potential to change our fundamental assumptions about life. Convinced of this I have set out to make sense of the phenomenon, keeping in mind the needs of two important groups of readers. This is a serious book, but I wanted it to be free enough of professional jargon to be accessible to educated lay-readers, many of whom may benefit in health by being released from the strait-jacket of Western biomedical concepts and practices. In addition, my teaching experience, in New Zealand and around the world, tells me that the material is both novel and relevant for otherwise orthodox clinicians (in a variety of disciplines) who see the need but lack confidence in venturing towards more holistic practice, because they lack a *coherent conceptual basis* for so doing. I write then also as a clinician keeping in mind the needs of clinicians.

To help with our explorations, material will be drawn from a variety of disciplines. I am not a trained philosopher, physicist, theologian, linguist, or sociologist. I am a physician, and a psychotherapist. I have spent the last twenty years bridging body, mind, and spirit perspectives with many people suffering from chronic illness, many of whom have had little relief from biomedical approaches, and whose diseases have responded to a meanings approach. I have struggled to relinquish deeply held assumptions rooted in a narrow biomedical scientific training, itself rooted in a wider dualistic culture. I have had to yield to the evidence of my own eyes and ears. I have read extraordinarily helpful things from disciplines and sources never considered by my peer physicians to be relevant to good clinical practice or treatment of disease. I have seen so many cases now of meaning-*full* disease that I know the phenomenon is universal. I realize the juggernaut of biomedicine will charge on for a while yet, but this book will help some patients and doctors, in tow with the juggernaut, struggling with diseases without really satisfactory clinical outcomes, to consider an approach which adds another dimension and yet does not need to be in competition with biomedicine properly practiced.

Ultimately, the book is about the nature of meaning, the relationship of meaning to the body, and the way in which meaning expresses itself in our health or lack of it. In another way it is about the conjunction of mind, body, and spirit. In a more practical perspective, the message is that meaning-full disease does make sense, that we do have a sound basis for a holism that includes meaning, and that we had better sort out our models of healthcare if we want to be the sorts of clinicians and healers our patients and clients deserve.

My first book, *Somatic Illness and the Patient's Other Story. A Practical Integrative Mind/Body Approach to Disease for Doctors and Psychotherapists* (Broom 1997), was about managing the realities of meaning-*full* disease in the cauldron of the clinical consultation, *so that patients could benefit.* This second book is about making *conceptual sense* of the phenomenon.

There are two core elements. The first element is the collection of meaning-full diseases presented here. Without this element there would be little justification for writing. These stories stand powerfully in their own right, demanding to be explained; we need to know 'how come'? The content of the stories proffered primarily emphasizes the element of *meaning-fullness*, rather than issues of *clinical management.* The focus is upon *phenomena*, and proceeding from there to principles, ideas, theory, philosophy, and models of disease, rather than upon diagnosis, categorization of meaning-full disease, and clinical skills.

That brings us to the second core element in the book, which is the inclusion and integration of many kinds of knowledge, perspective, and insight available in other traditions and academic disciplines that help us make sense of the phenomenon.

The final chapter briefly addresses possible spiritual underpinnings to meaning-full disease. Considering the potential size of this topic the chapter is admittedly rather brief, but it does summarize the core of my current thinking. It is an area of active exploration for me, and I hope that the chapter will be the fore-runner of a future volume.

The writing has at times been difficult, even exhausting. Some territories conceded access easily, but others did not. At times I despaired of being able to crystallize difficult concepts in the brief communicative manner required by the sort of book I set out to write. And yet the hard times have been interspersed with periods of quiet satisfaction, and sometimes triumph. In the fragmented world of healthcare the integrative task is difficult. I do hope that this book offers not only encouragement to people looking for whole person care, but also provides a solid sense that we can with justification demand and provide such care.

In a profound sense, patients are both the beginning and the end of my work, and this book would be a relatively sterile, theoretical, abstract document if it were not continually grounded in the stories of the many patients who have sought consultation and on-going clinical care and therapy with me, and with the psychotherapists who work with me. Without exception, the discussions herein are inspired by what I have seen, learned, and struggled with in my clinic. In the Western medical ethos, integrative mind/body clinical work is challenging and frequently extremely difficult, certainly for the clinician, and even more often for the patient. I know that, in using an integrative mind/body approach, I have enabled many people to find healing, but it is also true to say that these same people have taught me an enormous amount about life, and about some of the less well-known or acknowledged processes that under-gird healing.

In every clinical case presented, I have gone to great lengths to remove or change identifying detail, without distorting the essentials of the clinical story. Therefore, similitude to someone known to a reader can be regarded as coincidence, or, perhaps more likely, a reflection of the commonness of the phenomenon described. In certain cases, where the story is for some reason very distinctive, even when identifying details have been altered, I have obtained written consent from the patients concerned.

Michael Harlow, Mark Murphy, John Elliott, and Sarah Broom critiqued the manuscript, in part or in full, in its middle to late stages of preparation. Their comments were most helpful, and their enthusiasm for the content even more so.

Finally, Alison, my companion on the journey for so many years, has been unremittingly supportive, encouraging, tolerant, and helpful. A simple 'thank you' bespeaks a great volume of gratitude.

CHAPTER ONE

The phenomena

We begin with *stories*, laying out in full view some of the raw, vivid associations that we see between personal experience and physical disease. The common phenomena of meaning-*full* diseases constitute powerful evidence that the nature of persons, and the diseases of real persons, involve much more than that which is implied by the ordinary practice of Western medicine and science. No matter how we twist and turn, trying to make sense of these phenomena, the truth is that our current biomedical assumptions cannot account for the expression of highly specific and personal meanings in bodily disease, at times with extraordinarily obvious symbolic features. These phenomena communicate as stories, speaking powerfully for a much more holistic way of 'seeing' ourselves as patients, and demanding a radical re-thinking of clinical practice by Western biomedical clinicians.

The stories are extremely varied. In some, the meaning is so obvious that the observer is stopped in his tracks. In others, the meaning is at first invisible or obscure; the observer must peek and pry a little, lift up this stone, and then another, and the meaning becomes obvious. Throughout the book I refer to many different kinds of story, but I will start with one that is middle-of-the-road, at the less spectacular end of the meaning-*full* disease spectrum. The detail of this story suggests that there is a strong connection between the clinical activity or severity of the patient's rheumatoid arthritis and the problems she experiences in close relationship:

***

Natalie is a forty-five year-old business woman. She was referred by her general practitioner because of a two year history of crippling arthritis (technically labeled 'sero-negative rheumatoid arthritis') affecting the hands, wrists, knees, and ankles. She had seen rheumatologists in two cities, and had received a wide range of the medical therapies available. She had developed life-threatening bone marrow problems as a complication of gold injection treatment. During the first consultation with me I confirmed the very typical appearances of rheumatoid arthritis in her joints. She was requiring constant steroid treatment to keep active. She was alarmed at the side-effects of drug treatments and wanted a second opinion and an alternative approach, if there was one.

I had nothing in the way of medications to offer her, so I turned to an exploration of her 'story.' Natalie revealed that she was adopted, but knew little about her biological parents. She had discovered her adoption through neighbors and relatives, and the only direct communication about it during her childhood, and since, was once when her mother screamed out "you are bloody adopted." Natalie's comment upon this was "that we don't talk about things that really matter." The other main theme, which had become much more apparent over the recent two to three years, was a need to be separate and free and have her own personal domain, and a feeling that the 'shared domain' takes over. She felt stuck in relationships with old friends, and that she somehow had to live out patterns that were no longer relevant. It reached something of a crisis at a certain Christmas, which she felt obliged to spend with these friends, though she was bored, and wanted to move onto something freer, something more true to her interests and reality. It is noteworthy that her arthritis originally began between that same Christmas and New Year. The same issues of stuck-ness were revealed in many aspects of her relationship with her partner, George. She saw him as stopping her from doing many things. She had taken a job at another town so that she could both hold on to the relationship and spend time out of it. But the problem remained unresolved because every new context quickly became a 'rut' as well. She said she was frustrated with her arthritis principally "because it stops me."

While my approach is always to start from the patient's story and try and discern the patterns that emerge, I did have some rudimentary preconceptions of what kind of story *might* be behind this sort of physical disorder. During my assessment of Natalie I recalled comments made by the psychoanalyst Joyce McDougall, the author of *Theatres of the Body* (1989), concerning the manifestations of rheumatoid arthritis as a reflection of unresolved conflicts around dependence and independence. I had also seen several previous patients, with rheumatoid arthritis, where a similar dynamic seemed to be crucial, and, given the material emerging in my initial session with Natalie, I felt I had a logic for exploring her story further along these lines.

Because she had to travel a considerable distance, I saw her only thirteen times over a period of eighteen months. Ten months after the sessions started she moved permanently to another town, in the process of which she formally separated from her husband, but with whom she continued a good friendship. At regular intervals she assessed her joint symptoms by rating the problem statement "*I have stiff painful swollen joints*" on a 0–8 scale. This 0–8 scale measures whether the "*problem upsets me and/or interferes with my normal activities.*" The scale is as follows: 0 = does not, 2 = slightly/sometimes, 4 = definitely/often, 6 = markedly/often, 8 = very severely/continuously. At the beginning of therapy she rated the state of her joints as grade 6. By fourteen months her joint symptoms were greatly improved, and she rated herself at grade 3. At eighteen months we stopped the sessions because she felt in reasonable health, though not entirely free of symptoms, and she certainly felt much freer in her life, with new horizons. At our last session together, she promised to write to me sometime to let me know how things turned out long-term (vide infra).

I turn now to the pervasive themes of our sessions together, which are most clearly and persuasively captured in her own words. On freedom and constraint: "*it's keeping me in a bind like my parents were," "I can't get moving," "I can't go out temporarily, or I will go back and be captured by the comfort zone," "comfort … is deathly … a lack of life … closed to new directions," "I want to loosen up.*" On feeling tied to her partner: "*I am responsible for his happiness," "it's hard to take freedom," "George still wants me," "I feel tethered, enslaved."* On who she is: *"I don't belong anywhere," "I don't know who I am, or what I want," "I lose me in relationship,"* I *was quite strong in asserting me as a child, but I've stopped asserting me," "I've got pathetic in the last five years."* On her geography: *"I hate being in (her town), it cripples me."*

Six years later, having had no contact in the interim, I received the promised letter out of the blue. She was doing remarkably well: *"I swim and bike regularly"* … *"I feel good"* … *"I hardly get sick"* … *"new health and happiness"* … *"direct result of my sessions with you"* … *"I think of the way you wouldn't accept my bullshit i.e., the image of myself that I had chosen to construct which you saw as somehow not congruent with something truer or more real about myself"* … *"It was very difficult to leave George, but I knew I needed to, years before really"* … *"I love living on my own … (George and I) "have a good friendship,"* … *"I was really glad I talked to my Mum about being adopted about six years ago … as a result of seeing you. …"*

***

For many people the notion of meaning-*full* diseases is sheer provocation. Are we really to believe that many of the physical diseases afflicting nice people have anything to do with emotional factors, or arise out of their meaning-*full stories?* One in six adults in New Zealand have arthritis: Surely I am not suggesting that something akin to Natalie's story applies in all these cases? The stories provided in this book, and in my previous writings, suggest that just as 'story' or subjective factors pervade our humanness, so they pervade our diseases. The great deceit of Western physico-materialistic medicine is that our diseases are separate from who we are and what we experience, separate from our stories. This is not so. The primary goal then is to show that the meaning-*fullness* of disease does make sense, that it is something we have to take seriously, and that if we do so we create huge potential for healing and clinical practice.

How did I get myself into this complex and controversial area? There is a story there as well. I have always been interested in synthesis and integration, but for a long time my work with patients was grounded in all the ordinary views and assumptions of medical students and doctors trained in the twentieth century. Indeed my perspectives were at the most scientific end of the medical spectrum given my training as a medical specialist in clinical immunology and my role as a medical school academic and clinician. But change began when, in the early 1980s, I abandoned immunology for training in psychiatry and then psychotherapy. The under-girding drive was towards a more integrative and holistic perspective, in respect of persons in general and, particularly, patients with illness. I did not know where I was going, except that the journey was exploratory and step-by-step. I had no pre-formed ideas or inklings of the meanings of physical disease beyond the conceptualizations of modern Western medicine.

A crucial step occurred in 1987, when I took the decision to combine my clinical immunology and psychotherapy trainings and roles into one integrated clinical practice. Thus, after a break of five years, I was again functioning as an allergist and clinical immunologist treating patients with physical symptoms of many different kinds. But this time it was different. I was also there as a trained psychotherapist. *Two* clinical perspectives and skill-sets influenced my consultations, and I was unable (and unwilling) to leave either of them outside the consulting room door.

I have described elsewhere (Broom 1997, 2000, 2002) the practical and clinical consequences of this new situation, both for patients and for my own personal practice. As I integrated my medical and psychotherapy practices I started seeing phenomena that had previously been invisible to me. I noticed that people presenting with physical diseases often had *stories* to match. Disease appeared *meaning-full*, rather than just *meaningful* for the sufferer. Initially I was stunned, and discomforted, partly because it was all new to me and partly because I did not know what to do with what I was seeing.

Over time, working with people from a combined mind/body perspective I discovered two important things. Firstly, meaning-*full* diseases are not rare, and they include florid physical diseases, not just those illnesses commonly thought of as 'psychosomatic.' I no longer believe there is substantial justification for dividing illness and disease into one group that is 'psychosomatic' and another group in which we can legitimately ignore 'mind' factors. Secondly, the meaning-*fullness* of all kinds of disease is relevant at a very practical level, because attention to meanings aspects leads to significant new therapeutic options for health professionals, and to a horizon of hitherto unimagined healing possibilities for the patient. This positive healing aspect has been dealt with at length in my previous writings, but is further illustrated in the cameo case histories provided throughout this book.

With these prefatory remarks behind us, let's continue with more case histories so that there is no doubt as to the nature of the phenomena upon which our discussions are based:

***

Emily, age 35, a landscape designer in a rural town, had suffered from very severe psoriasis, a disfiguring skin condition, for seventeen years, and covering most parts of her body. It had been unresponsive to all types of orthodox medical approach including potent immunosuppressive drugs. Her illness began when she was rejected by her first boy-friend in preference for one of her close friends. As the initial session progressed, I began to see the beginnings and the fluctuations of her illness in terms of the vicissitudes of intimate relationship, and referred her to a mind-body-oriented psychotherapist. Initially Emily was reluctant and sceptical, but by the fourth session became very engaged in the work. Within less than ten sessions of psychotherapy her psoriasis remitted. I received a letter of thanks from her saying how delighted she was with her improvement. She claimed that not once in the seventeen years had she had a remission anything like this. At around the eighth session of her psychotherapy she returned to me for a medical certificate, and, at that point, the only residues of her psoriasis were some hardly perceptible, oval, dusky, pigmented patches on one flank.

I took the opportunity to ask *her*, and, later, her therapist, to conceptualize what had happened. They both agreed it had to do with *boundaries*, with taking on board other peoples' feelings, of getting 'too involved.' Any stirring up of such issues led to an almost immediate onset of burning and itchiness in her skin lesions. There were additional important questions of whether she was 'attractive' or not; whether she was 'supersensitive' or, conversely, whether 'nothing offends me'; or whether she was 'free' or 'forced into a mould.'

A year later I came across her by chance in a library. She bounced up to me, baring her right elbow, to show a small area of psoriasis four centimeters in diameter which had flared during a recent stressful tussle with local town authorities over a major commissioned landscape design, but otherwise her skin had remained clear.

***

What are the mindbody correlations here? It does not take much discernment to define Emily's major personal themes as having to do with 'boundary-making,' 'visual attractiveness,' 'sensitivity and insensitivity,' and being forced into a 'mould,' and that such themes have an obvious natural physical correlate in the skin. Chiozza (1998, and to whom we will return in chapter five), in discussing meaning-*full* skin disease, emphasizes that the skin is not merely a necessary 'coating' on a biological mechanism; it is also a 'barrier,' and a 'contact surface' mediating touch. Touch helps us define ourselves in relation to the external world including other persons. In this sense the skin is the *bodily representation* of the felt barrier between the experiencing organism and the external world. We talk of people being thick or thin-skinned, when we speak of their abilities to resist slight or insult. And the skin is the physical representation of our experience of ourselves as having a boundary between our *inner* world and our *outer* world. The skin is of course more than a barrier; for example, it helps constitute us as *containers*. We ingest into it and excrete from it. If the skin is damaged we bleed from it.

Returning to Emily's experience of herself, we find she wrestles with boundaries, and with being forced into someone else's 'mould.' She is too easily 'touched' by other people's feelings. Significantly, when she starts to deal with these issues her psoriasis clears. Her psoriasis appears to represent conflicts regarding these boundary issues. We might even call her skin disturbance a physical *metaphor* for these issues. In chapter three we will present in detail the case for *somatic metaphors*, describing and discussing many more and quite varied physical disease manifestations that appear to be specific, exquisitely appropriate, physical representations of the sufferer's subjective experience *in* the world, and *of* the world. But Emily's psoriasis is a typical example of the kind of meaning-*full* disease I see every day.

I am, of course, not the first person to draw attention to these phenomena. I will refer to other important figures in chapters three and seven, but Georg Groddeck (1866–1934) was an early pioneer who has a sentimental appeal for me. He was a German physician who wrote extensively about the meaning of illness, and when I discovered his writings, late in my own integrative journey, I felt relieved, reassured, saddened, and discouraged. Here was a courageous physician, remote from me in time, distance, and culture, seeing and describing the same clinical phenomena. That was heartening. On the other hand Groddeck experienced hostility and opposition from the medical and psychoanalytic establishments, and I resonated with the difficulty he had in challenging the mind/body dualism of clinical practice. I have to say, though, that I have mostly experienced resistance rather than hostility.

Groddeck's theorizing around his cases of meaning-*full* disease has little appeal for me, but his cases are vivid and timeless. One of these (Groddeck, see Schact 1928, pp. 208–210) involved a man who, as a teenager,

***

.'..was taught shoe-making by the village shoe-maker ... Among those who came to the shop was a certain blind man whom all the village people called a blasphemer of God ... (who) made an unforgettable impression on the boy. After a time (the boy) gave up shoe-making ... for he was suffering from retinal haemorrhage, and the doctor warned him he must find some other work less trying to the eyes. Years later he came to consult me ... his eyes had gradually got worse ... the oculist had told him nothing more could be done for him. The retinal haemorrhage was continually starting anew ... autumn was the worst time for the haemorrhage, and he also suffered from great depression in autumn as now-in October ... I asked him whether anything serious had ever happened to him in October, but he said there was nothing. As I was not convinced, I asked him to name any number, and he gave me 'eight.' To my further question whether anything had happened to him when he was eight years old, he again replied in the negative. At that point it occurred to me that he had told me how the blind man was called a blasphemer of God, so I asked him whether he had ever blasphemed God. He laughed and said he had been very pious as a child, but for many years now he had ceased to trouble himself about these things. God and the Church, they were only bogies used to deceive the common people. Suddenly he stammered, grew pale and fell back in his chair unconscious.

When he came to himself again he fell weeping on my neck, saying: "Doctor, you are right. I am a blasphemer of God, just as the blind man was, of whom I told you. I have never told a single soul about it, not even in confession, and now when I think of it, I find it almost unbearable. And you are right too about the autumn, and about my being eight years old. It all happened in autumn in the year I was eight. In my home district, which is strictly Catholic, there are wooden crucifixes on the borders between one village and another. At one such crucifix we, my brothers and I and a few other boys, were throwing stones, when I was so unfortunate as to knock the figure of Christ from the crucifix so that it fell and broke into pieces. That is the most terrible experience in the whole of my life."

***

After their consultative relationship began, Groddeck and his patient explored together two episodes of eye haemorrhage, and found they related in one instance to getting on a tram at a place where a crucifix stood, and in the other instance

***

to the sight of an iron cross worn by an ex-soldier. This cleared up, and from that time, thirteen years ago, no haemorrhages have occurred. Yet now he is a book-keeper and must use his eyes more than most people.

***

This kind of conjunction between meaning and florid physical disease had become increasingly unimaginable to the modern Western medical mind rooted in physico-materialism and rationalism (and we will address that crucial issue in various ways in later chapters). Therefore it is not really surprising that, despite his pioneering efforts, Groddeck slipped from view (until his writings were re-published in the psychoanalytic literature in the 1980s). Twentieth century medical practice became increasingly dominated by the mechanistic premises of biomedicine, and its modernist disavowal of anything with a whiff of the metaphysical. And yet, despite these powerful forces, it was not possible to rid medicine completely of the idea that human subjectivity plays a role in disease, and it kept emerging in a number of guises (see chapter two).

As we will see, many people are recognizing that giving subjectivity its proper place demands a view of people that is unitary rather than divided, a view which allows both the objective and subjective aspects of our personhood to be mutually present, in the same time and space. Neither is seen to subjugate the other. We will discover that the very existence of meaning-*full* disease underscores the fact that the apparent separation between physical disturbance and the subjective 'story,' with all its personal and community meanings, is something we *do* to the patient/client; it is something we impose on reality. Let's now look at a clinical example that demonstrates clearly some of the foolishness, and waste of time and other resources, that we can get into when we separate the minds and bodies of our patients.

*****

Peter, aged 30, presented with ten years of severe back pain following an injury sustained during a mountaineering expedition. Extensive and varied attempts at treatment and rehabilitation had failed. General physical activity, sexual intercourse, and sleep were profoundly affected. He had not worked for the ten years since the original injury, except for occasional very brief and unsuccessful forays into jobs ultimately found to be unsuitable. Surgery had been recommended because magnetic resonance scanning showed lumbar four and five disc narrowing, disc dessication, and oedema in adjacent vertebra. He had refused this option, terrified that it might lead to even more disability.

During the first consultation, while we talked, he lay on the floor being unable to sit on an ordinary chair. The other most obvious features were the exquisite tenderness of his back muscles on examination, his profound suspicion of me, and his huge anger towards his third party funding source.

His 'story' can be told another way. He was (in his view) the unwelcome last-born of numerous children, and the only one who had failed academically. He established his self-esteem through sporting prowess. As a child his angry temperament was notorious, to the extent that he was given a special nickname (not disclosed here) to reflect this. He left school early, with a strong sense of academic failure, which he compensated for by *excellence in sport*. The 'broken back' caused by the mountaineering accident symbolized the destruction of his capacity for sporting excellence, of his worth and competency. In his view, surgery on his back might just *complete* the crippling process. Thus surgery was a terrifying prospect. Because of his pain he was unable to re-establish himself in any sort of sporting activity. As a person who was an academic failure he could not imagine developing alternative non-physical 'head' skills to replace his loss of physical competence. He was enraged with his funding organization because of the pressures they put on him, and afraid they would terminate his support, and leave him stranded. They and the various medical specialists concerned with his care were almost entirely focused on his physical body, and had no understanding whatsoever of what was going on in his subjectivity. Not only was the latter divided off, it was also invisible.

After acting as a mediator with his third-party funding source I did nine sessions with Peter. My notes give some idea of the process: 'We have both found the intensity of the encounters almost intolerable.' He raged on endlessly about his funding institution. It was extremely difficult to get him to focus on his anger issues, and how his anger might be perpetuating his back pain. At the ninth session, in utter frustration, I informed him I could not work with him unless he agreed to stop talking about his problems with the funding source, and focused more upon the role of his anger in his back pain. I thought I had lost him but he returned three weeks later, willing to stop focusing upon the funding source. A remarkable process of change ensued. Seven sessions later he was running his own business, which involved considerable physical activity. He was continuing to get some minor pain if he did too much lifting, but he was essentially living a normal life.

***

This story emphasizes the need to regain our ability to see people as 'wholes,' and to expand the medical focus to include the subjective. Doing so leads to a radical therapeutic shift, the end-result for Peter being a return to work after years of State-dependency. This was achieved by shifting from looking at Peter as an (injured mechanistic) *object* to Peter as an angry *subject*. I will return to Peter's story (and his own account of what happened) in chapter ten.

Meaning-*full* diseases force us to consider the relationships between conceptual categories such as *experience, meaning, language, body, mind,* and, of course, *disease.* The issues that arise are very complex, and this is starkly highlighted when we consider meaning-*full* diseases in children, especially infants before they develop language, a subject I regard as crucial to any theory of meaning-*full* disease. A clinical case sharpens up the dilemmas much more quickly than does wordy abstraction:

***

Jane is four years old, and lost all her hair (alopecia) ten months before I saw her with her parents. A story unfolded, focused around an older brother who had been stillborn. Jane was conceived in an understandable ethos of ongoing parental dread that something tragic might also happen to her. She was born of a complicated premature delivery, and was a 'colicky' infant, also diagnosed as having 'reflux.' She was very unwilling to separate from her parents, and was difficult to settle in childcare. She liked structure, rules, and certainty, a pattern that I interpreted as reflecting her underlying anxiety. When Jane was age three the family shifted house, and this seemed to increase her separation anxiety. Ten months before I saw her, when she was age three and a half, her father went on an academic field trip to South America, and on his return home Jane's mother immediately went off to attend a school reunion. Coincidentally, Jane's primary carer at the day care facility fractured a leg and was unable to work. The staff reported that during that week (whilst both Mother and primary care-giver were away) Jane 'climbed the wall' in her behavior. Jane's hair started to fall out. It grew back in during the summer holidays when both Mother and Father were around and she was not attending day-care. It fell out again when the work year began for the parents and Jane started with a new pre-school.

***

We will return to Jane's story again in chapter six when we explore the relationship between communication and disease, but some things are usefully signalled here. The categories of experience and meaning are not ultimately dependent on language, though they are greatly enlarged by it. New-born infants cannot talk, but they do have experiences. We struggle to discern the exact nature of those experiences but whether we understand them or not they are definitely *experiencing*. Returning to Jane, I would say that her alopecia signifies, in an 'embodied' manner, her 'experience' of loss, which is, in turn, rooted in the family experience of loss.

The phenomena of meaning-*full* diseases suggest that the categories of mind, body, meaning, experience, and language are interpenetrating, entangled, reciprocal, and mutually sustaining. But the observer can divide them. I look at a person from one angle and I see 'body.' I take a step sideways, and 'look' from another angle, and I see 'story.' Another case history provides a vivid demonstration of this:

***

Margaret, age 44, was referred for depression triggered when she was embraced by her church minister who was clearly sexually aroused. When aged 15, her twin brother sexually assaulted her, beginning with a demand that she expose her breasts, and going on to forceful vaginal penetration. She was left bleeding and traumatized. During therapy we uncovered almost unutterable feelings in relation to this trauma, and collaterally she developed excessive bleeding from the uterus. She was thoroughly investigated by a gynecologist, and eventually had a hysterectomy. Within a few weeks she started to pass blood in her urine. Despite further investigation by a urologist the source of this bleeding was never found, and she continued to periodically pass blood in the urine, especially at times when she felt badly treated by powerful males (in her financial-services work-place). But this was not the end of the phenomena. She then developed bleeding from both her breasts. Again she was thoroughly investigated and nothing sinister was found. Margaret and I realized from early on that the bleeding from the breasts commenced at the time we were exploring her feelings towards her brother who raped her.

***

In this story, body, relationship, experience, and disease are clearly very entangled. The original rape 'experience' and Margaret's presentation, nearly three decades later, have vivid physical and subjective elements. Powerlessness, loneliness, fragmentation, fear, rage, physical bleeding from the genital and urinary tracts, and the breasts, are all mixed up together—both then and now. Despite the passage of many years, Margaret's body seems once again able to represent the 'experience' in a symbolic way, reminiscent of the original rape episode.

To understand this interpenetration of experience and disease we must go beyond ordinary biomedical concepts, drawing upon a number of useful modern ideas and findings. I will refer in later chapters to the work and ideas of Alfred North Whitehead, David Bohm, David Chalmers, and David Griffin, who, all, in one way or another, assert that the world isn't just static spatial matter, but is an energy system manifested in stable, or semi-stable patterned structures. Our bodies are therefore *structured energy forms*, and the capacity for 'experience' is a fundamental quality or potential. If this is true, we come very close to the idea that the patterned structured energy forms carry not only physical structure but also experience, and ultimately therefore meanings, pushing towards a view of disease as the emergence of a new dysfunctional form that has both physical and 'experience' dimensions.

Such ideas, and many more (which we will explore later), embolden me to assert that Margaret, the person, should be seen as a *richly structured and patterned semi-stable energy form*. This form entails a *patterned physicality*, the *body*, which includes the uterus, urinary tract, and breasts. This form also entails an intensely *experiential 'story'* (involving these same organs) of rape, a violation that brings *new damaging information* to the whole. The rape 'experience' is *structured into* the energy form, powerfully *re-setting the patterns*. The *'shape'* and *vitality* of her patterned structures are affected and undermined by the rape episode, and eventually they *cannot be sustained*. In the end it is the minister's betrayal of her trust that triggers a *collapse*, and with the collapse comes *illness* and *disease*. Depression appears. Eventually the rape 'experience' reappears in both physical (bleeding) and subjective (powerful feelings) forms, and for health to be reinstated in her patterned structures the damage has to be repaired in some way.

In this first chapter I have emphasized the vital substrate of this book, the phenomena of meaning-*full* disease. I have also hinted at some of the issues that arise and which must be explored more deeply and systematically if we are to make sense of it all. That is the task engaged in the remaining chapters.

CHAPTER TWO

Colliding mind-sets

It is important to emphasize that in the notion of meaning-*full* disease I am not focusing upon the numerous meanings that ill-nesses have for sufferers *after* they become established. Those kinds of meanings are understood by everybody, and are common-ly expressed by patients in such questions as "why me?" or "what have I done to deserve this?" or, for example, in the deep disap-pointment of having to give up, because of injury, a sport around which an athlete has constructed his identity and self-esteem. All ill-nesses have powerful or significant meanings, in the sense of having emotional impact and consequences.

The meanings of meaning-*full* disease are those that actually pre-dispose us to illness, that contribute powerfully to the onset of ill-ness, and that play an important role in keeping illness going. They are both personal and shared meanings and stories that play a piv-otal role in the emergence of physical disease. They are not just those meanings that emerge for us when we are afflicted with some inex-plicable change for the worse in our biological machinery.

It is important to confront, in some detail, the reality that the thinking of many people is so saturated with physico-materialist assumptions about life and reality that the idea of meaning-*full*

disease is shocking. The notion of disease rooted in personal meaning does *not* make sense to people imbued with the typical Western
mind-set. Let's ground the discussion of this in two examples of real
meaning-*full* diseases, to avoid a drift to arm-chair theorizing.

***

Mary first develops headaches at age thirteen when her father
dies. The headaches persist for six months. At age seventeen
when a boy-friend breaks off with her she develops the same
type of headache, again lasting for six months. At twenty-one
she falls pregnant, and the father of the child abandons her. The
headaches resume and persist for the next twelve years, triggered from day to day and week to week by issues of relationship with males. The point of Mary's story is that her headaches
appear to be triggered by important males leaving or betraying
her. The symptom seems to be specifically connected with this
theme, which builds in intensity over time. Mary did not want to
hear this, and was angry with the suggestion that her headaches
might be related to unresolved feelings. For her this implied her
headaches were not 'real,' that they were imaginary, and 'all in
the head.' She broke off further contact with me.

George has suffered a very severe rash on his face for forty
years. He has had repeated treatments with steroid drugs and
has developed marked side effects from these. The rash began
soon after a bitter family argument involving other family members who (in his view) cheated him out of inheriting the family
farm. He retaliated by buying the farm next door and, thus, the
injustice *"was constantly in my face"* (his exact words). The rash
cleared whenever he took time away from the farm. The point of
George's story is that both his words and his body (his face)
seem to be telling us about his anger or bitterness at being the
victim of injustice or cheating. George quickly accepted this conceptualization. It seemed to be a relief to have an explanation
that made sense.

***

These two patients respond in opposite ways. Mary's response may
of course reflect the possibility that I was wrong in my interpretation, but I think it was more than that. There were at least two issues:
one was that she saw the interpretation as making her headaches
less 'real'; another was the fear of re-visiting the pain of the early

losses and rejections. George had neither of those problems. He was just grateful to establish a reason, and work from there. Clearly, the notion of meaning-*full* disease evokes very different responses in individual patients, and I may have to work quite hard with some people to overcome cultural and personal resistance to even looking at the possibility. It is one thing to grapple with the emerging conceptual issues in a book that one can write or read at leisure; it is a very different matter working out the implications of meaning-*full* disease in time-constrained clinics faced with distressed patients, or in the cauldron of a medical conference presenting the argument for meaning-*full* disease to one's sceptical colleagues, who, until such moments, have never even considered the possibility that many chronic illnesses might be rooted in meaning. Such encounters demand clarity of thought and language.

Whilst I never *assume* how any of my patients will react to the idea of meaning-*full* disease, there are several stereotypical reaction patterns and attitudes to disease, observable in our Western cultural context, which those of us who work in this area repeatedly come up against. I am going to lay these out in some detail and, by so doing, construct a socio-cultural context for our further explorations and discussions. To some degree, it is the assumptions underlying these typical patterns that make the explorations in this book necessary.

The first reaction pattern is that of many of my medical colleagues, who practice 'modern' medicine by focusing almost entirely on the physical aspects of their patients. Their approach to disease can be termed *physicalist*. As already mentioned, the rather general notion of 'stress' contributing to health breakdown is, for many of them, an acceptable concept, but the more specific notion of a meaning-*full* 'story' leading to an exquisitely 'appropriate' meaning-*full* disease is utterly foreign, even ludicrous. In their view, diseases are more or less construed as inevitable 'mechanical' breakdowns of biological machines in a difficult world. The materialist paradigm that ultimately underpins this view is the *'standard scientific view of nature ... that it is composed of "dead matter" – so that even living systems are ultimately composed of unfeeling, purposeless, meaningless atoms embedded in equally unfeeling, purposeless, and meaningless fields of force'* (de Quincey 2002).

In the course of the twentieth century, these practitioners (and their patients) became accustomed to, besotted with, seduced by the efficacy and the tantalizing promises of modern technological medicine based on the standardized Western culture-wide materialist and physicalist approach to disease. Of course, this approach has made many very positive contributions to health care, and I employ some of them with my own patients. But many clinicians, practicing in healthcare systems, also feel that the reductionistic premises of biomedicine have adversely shaped and constrained the assumptions and intellectual lives of generations of medical and paramedical clinicians, and spawned an almost obsessive focus on the patient's mechanistic body to the exclusion of other elements.

The rise of this materialist and physicalist biomedical model has been paralleled by a general loss of 'soul' from clinical practice. By loss of soul I mean a relative loss of awareness of the importance to clinical outcomes of many aspects of the subjectivity of the patient and his/her family and social unit, of the interpersonal elements of good healthcare, and of the health-promoting and healing aspects of the clinician-patient relationship. At some level these medical colleagues 'know' that these elements *are* relevant to health care and healing, but they are very difficult to measure, and are therefore side-lined or ignored in a biomedical ethos that, at its worst, will honor measurable trivia above un-measurable but otherwise crucial elements.

One crucial element of 'soul' is the human experience of *meaning*. Of course most clinicians would acknowledge the centrality of meaning in peoples' lives. I have come across some interesting paradoxes. For example, one only has to enquire regarding the private interests of physicians to discover the emphasis many of them put on literature, music, and art. I have noted that these same physicalist doctors may have family members with interests in psychotherapy and even in the 'unscientific' alternative therapies. The public 'face' may be different to the private reality. A few years ago I attended a medical social function in Australia, and got into conversation with the wife of a medical specialist well-known for his espousal of evidence-based medicine, and for publicly-stated skepticism regarding mindbody matters. The woman showed some interest in my clinical orientation and work, and commented that I and her husband would have much in common because he " … has several shelves of books at home about psychology and so on." Her husband overheard this exchange, and, turning to him, I expressed my surprise.

He seemed discomforted, and said "There are some things it is better for colleagues not to know." The physicalist view of disease dom-
inates medicine, and physicians feel at risk if they are seen not to
conform.

All of us are fascinated and preoccupied with meanings. Our
lives are governed by them. But, despite this, meanings and 'soul'
are assumed to have little relevance to the diseases we see in our
clinics. Can this really be true? What are the implications for biomedicine if we bring disease and meaning together? Why do we
hesitate to look at the possibilities of doing so? What are we afraid
of? Why do many patients look more willingly at meaning in their
illnesses than do their doctors? How is it that so often patients know
that they are ill because of this or that event or circumstance, but
have never discussed this aspect with their doctors?

Doctors have become biotechnologists. Over this last century we
have seen physicians transform from being reassuring healers, pur-
veying mostly doubtful remedies, to become highly trained technical specialists of the body, human repositories of burgeoning, even
crushing, levels of information. It is a crude generalization, but this
profession, to which I have been committed since boyhood, has
moved inexorably from a place where the balance was dominantly a
healing ethos with a small amount of technical ability, to a place
where the balance is dominantly technical ability with a relatively
small amount of healing ethos. It is a place where physicalism and
scientism are joint-emperors. In this empire patients cannot disclose
their private hunches about the meaning of their illnesses to their
doctors without risking impatience, disbelief, scorn, or humiliation.

Those who work entirely from physicomaterialist assumptions
will say this biotechnological emphasis is entirely appropriate. In
their view doctors *are* disease technologists, and we had better get
used to it. It is the way things are. Certainly this biomedical perspective is dominant in the Western world, and entrenched within the
power structures of the medical profession, and the legitimatising
vehicles of peer review, quality control and re-accreditation, and
fund management schemes and policies.

But are the patients in agreement? Patients are grateful for the
'miracles' that technology undoubtedly delivers, but many do not
agree with the physicalist assumptions that increasingly underpin
clinical practice. They want responses that are as much concerned

with *persons* as they are with *bodies-as-machines*. For most clinicians, the possibility of 'real' physical illnesses having their origins in the patients' personal 'stories' occurs only in those illnesses known by everybody to be 'psychosomatic,' or perhaps in illnesses or health mishaps like AIDS or alcohol-related accidents where psychosocial factors are obvious. But these are the exceptions, distinct illness categories separate from the majority of physical diseases that are seen as *purely* physical. Therefore it is hard for clinicians, often pressured for time and deeply immersed in a *bodies-as-machines* model, to turn to patient data that is seen as essentially irrelevant to the medical task. Whatever may be said to soften this appraisal, and however nice and kind medical practitioners are to their patients, it is unarguable that the eyes and ears of the medical profession are mostly tuned in to their patients' physical data and tuned out to personal 'story' data. The story data are invisible.

For most health professionals, physical disease is attributable to some misfortune of genetics, biochemistry, infection, toxicity, mutation, impact of lifestyle (unhealthy eating habits, lack of exercise etc.), and, as already mentioned, 'stress.' But, even if the concept of stress is allowed at the borders of these professionals' understandings, the notion that highly specific personal meanings give rise to disease remains, for many, incomprehensible and even offensive, violating entrenched assumptions about disease and illness, as well as about the nature of personhood and reality.

It is unfair to categorize all modern physicians as completely closed to the relevance of meaning in disease. Recently, I attended a physicians' medical education meeting. A cardiologist presented the case of a man with a 'heart attack.' He began by telling us that the patient, an ardent supporter of a local sports team, had been watching a finals game with a relative visiting from another city, from which the opposing team had also come. The visiting team won the important game. Immediately after the game a fierce argument developed between the patient and his visiting relative, and the local man developed chest pain, and was admitted to hospital with acute coronary obstruction. In his presentation, the cardiologist moved on to the technological aspects, showing some stunning videos of clot dissolution and removal. He concluded with a patient discharge plan solely comprised of treatment with several drugs, but no discussion with the patient regarding the argument associated with the onset of the event. In question time, the cardiologist was asked what he thought was the significance of the argument. He seemed rather embarrassed, and dismissively said: "*Oh, it's probably not relevant.*" But why did he include it in the presentation? Discussion revealed that this physicianly audience could not consider the association of the coronary event with the post-game argument as relevant unless an *understandable mechanism* could be proposed. To my mind the cardiologist was in a dilemma. He clearly thought it was relevant at an intuitive and common sense level, but he was also embarrassed because he could not speak to it at a level that would satisfy his biomedical colleagues, who tended to address the point dismissively and sceptically. To do him justice, he did include the 'fierce argument' data in the field of view. If this book has any relevance it will be to justify such data being in the field of view at all times.

The second group I am using here to help illustrate the variance in attitudes to meaning-*full* disease is comprised of people who consult me with a physical illness and who harbour a conviction that they are ill because of something important that has happened in their personal lives. They are not a large group, at least in my practice. A few come openly, determined to draw my attention to their hypothesis. But, mostly, they will not disclose their beliefs unless asked directly. If asked, one might say "*I've always wondered whether it had something to do with* … (one event or another)." Here is an example:

***

"*I know when it began … it was twenty minutes after my mother died.*" The man who made that statement had a very long history of diarrhoea characteristically occurring in bookshops and libraries, though that association had never been recorded or discussed in his many healthcare consultations over many years. It was invisible to the clinicians. The patient also *knew* that the diarrhoea was somehow connected to the death of his mother, but had never said this to his physicians. Careful enquiry led us to a memory of his mother destroying all his books when he was age ten, at a time when they shifted house. The connections between loss of books, loss of mother, diarrhoea, and collections of books in libraries or shops became very obvious. His rather vague awareness of the various connections meant he needed help to get to the underlying meanings.

**

These patients disregard science and biomedical orthodoxy and somehow know that they are sick *because* of the meaningful things that have occurred in their lives. They *know* that their stories and their illnesses are deeply entwined. Their knowledge is intuitive, circumstantial, and anecdotal—that 'dirty' word that has the power to destroy the credibility of just about anything that individual human beings observe. But these patients don't care about the problems surrounding the validity of anecdotes. They just *sense* the relationship between their illnesses and their stories.

If we are deeply committed to the biomedical view we can find all sorts of reasons to doubt the knowledge of these patients. We may question the science of their knowing. We may ascribe their belief to some subterranean motive, or to some psychologically understandable defensive structure. We might speculate that their knowing bespeaks some deep human requirement for making sense of the bad things that happen to us, when in reality there is no sense to be made. We might argue that they do not want to be left stranded with the implications of having a disease which has emerged for no deeper reason than that we are biological machines, machines that, like all machines, are prone to faulty construction, or wear and tear. We imagine they are driven to devise a reason for their illnesses. We could assume that in this particular sub-group of patients an unusually large burden of meaninglessness drives their knowing. We might even be really arrogant and lump them in with the ignorance of animist religion, or belief in flying saucers. And yet many of these patients are highly intelligent and educated people. I do accept that this sort of knowing may be grossly erroneous, like the 'knowing' of flat-earthers. But the comparison falls down immediately. Unlike flat-earth hypotheses there is a huge amount of evidence that mindbody connections are important in disease, and we will return to that later.

There is a third and much larger 'agnostic' grouping of people between these two extremes about whom, after years of including a meanings perspective in my work, I can make some fairly confident generalizations. Firstly, though they largely accept the dominant physicalist views of the medical profession, because that is all they have been exposed to, many of them intuitively understand, accept, and frequently welcome attention to personal story factors, though their positive responses are very dependent upon how skilful the clinician is in introducing such matters so that the patient does not feel stigmatized or blamed. An example of the sort of openness we see has come up in my practice as I write:

***

A 35 year old scientist and university teacher from Europe had suffered, as a child and teenager, severe allergic symptoms of the eyes and nose, which had been cured by allergy 'shots' or immunotherapy. Soon after arriving in New Zealand he fell prey to 'any bugs that came along.' He consulted me because each year, starting late autumn or early winter, he develops a very irritating drip from the back of his nose into his throat, requiring constant throat clearing. It usually cleared towards the end of the winter, though most recently it had continued right through the summer. Though he and his doctor had wondered whether his allergies had returned, the new symptoms were quite different. Allergy skin testing revealed that his original allergies had indeed disappeared. I said I believed the symptoms were not due to allergy. He asked me about alternative explanations. I told him some stories of patients whose sinus problems were rooted in personal life issues and meanings. He became thoughtful, and said that the way his job was constructed he felt chronically frustrated at not being able to get onto his research work and the writing of papers. What's more, this feeling reached its peak each year about the start of winter as his student responsibilities reached a peak. It subsided again to towards the end of the year. I agreed that this was an interesting association, but expressed puzzlement as to how this would explain his symptoms continuing through the recent summer. He flushed, and looked a little anxious, and then said '*Ah, I know what that was ... an unusual thing ... I had to go on a prolonged summer field trip, which competed with my other plans.*' He left saying '*Thank you, for a most interesting session.*'

***

Many people, like this scientist, respond very positively to something that makes sense, and especially if it opens up a route for healing that has few risks or side-effects. Consequently I find that very frequently my main role is education and making good sense of these connections between mind and body in the patient's illness. Making good sense to patients is crucial in the clinic, and it is the very objective of this book.

Secondly, many in this third group value the biomedical approach for what it can offer, but have no compunction in exploring the possibilities offered by other healing modalities which may be scorned by the medical profession. This implies many things. It underscores the reality that many people are not as confined in their assumptions as doctors are. They know there is more to life than that which can be measured, they are willing to be pragmatic in their explorations of a variety of possibilities, and they know they are not going to be led in these other directions by their doctors. Nevertheless we do have a responsibility to be very thoughtful about the non-biomedical alternatives that we offer patients. People who are ill or desperate for answers will be susceptible to dubious practice whatever its origins. This book is therefore an attempt to show the conceptual integrity of a clinical practice that allows meaning and disease, mindbody approaches and biomedical approaches, in the same 'space.'

Thirdly, in many circumstances we are expressing our 'stories' in illness and disease because the strands of meaning and their associated feelings, of which the stories are comprised, are too difficult to handle in other dimensions of personal expression. Therefore within this group there are patients for whom the story approach is very threatening. It takes time and skill to assist these people to a point where they can both accept a role for such meanings and resolve the associated emotional intensities sufficiently to make further expression in the body unnecessary.

I have previously emphasized (Broom 1997) that one of the major problems we have introducing meanings elements into a consultation is that some patients immediately assume that we are implying something negative. This gives rise to a variety of questions sometimes stated, sometimes not. One set of questions pivots around issues of responsibility and blame. Typical examples are: *"Are you saying I am making myself ill?"*; and *"Are you saying that a person with cancer is to blame for his/her illness, and ultimately his/her death?"* Other questions pivot around the mysteries of how different ways of looking at disease really do fit together. Typical examples are: *"What about genetic abnormalities?"* and *"What about infants who get ill?"* Other questions relate to issues of authenticity, reality, and madness. Typical examples are: *"So you think I am a hypochondriac?" "Are you saying it is all in my head?" "Do you think my symptoms aren't really real?"* and *"Are you really saying I am a nutter?"*

Most of these questions arise from an important sociocultural reality, that it is much more 'respectable' to have a completely physical illness than one rooted in meanings. Again, the reasons for this have been detailed previously (Broom 1997), but the result is that, apart from the unusually brave and resilient, or the patients with chronic illness who are absolutely desperate and will try anything, fears such as being labeled a "nutter" will drive many people away from acknowledging the role of their stories in their illnesses, and therefore, in many cases, lock them into chronic disease, recurrent ill health or multiple illnesses. Because of this it follows, and this is truly shocking, that the most popular models of disease actually *maintain* many illnesses and diseases. If we can re-work our assumptions about disease, so that patients find it possible to understand and acknowledge the inevitable role of their personal meanings (and the meanings of others) in their diseases, we will have achieved a great deal.

Meaning-*full* diseases in real patients is the springboard for all the discussions here. But there is one special kind of meaning-*full* disease that provides the most powerful justification for the exploration in this book. It is the phenomenon we call *somatic metaphor*, in which an exquisitely specific meaning is mirrored by an exquisitely 'appropriate' illness. This phenomenon has major implications for patients with actual diseases, for our notions of what a person is, for the future of medicine, and for our understanding of the nature of reality. We now turn to somatic metaphors.

CHAPTER THREE

Somatic metaphors

The phenomenon of *somatic metaphor* is the most striking example of the many ways in which meanings and other emotional and subjective elements may be demonstrated in physical disease processes. To begin I offer two examples, the first of which is a very obvious somatic metaphor. The second, while reasonably obvious, does require the observer to work a little harder to access the relationships between the patient's meanings and disease manifestation.

***

Eunice, a 71-year-old woman, had an 18-month history of generalized thickening of the skin, and tissues under the skin, causing uncomfortable splinting of the chest, and tightness of the arms and upper legs. This thickening was very obvious. Despite her age it was impossible to pinch her skin into folds. Despite intensive investigation a firm diagnosis had not been made. I will not emphasise the medical detail but though the appearances were not classical she was told she had "connective tissue disease" and was accordingly treated with steroids and other potent drugs.

27

I was asked to see her for a second opinion. I began by enquiring about the onset of her skin thickening. She startled me by saying that it began when she fell over in the local garden nursery, sustaining injuries to her face and legs. I was inclined to brush this information off, and get on with the important (sic) material. But something made me hesitate, and I enquired further. She described the fall as "*shattering*." Mystified as to the relevance of this I asked what effect this event had had on her. She replied: "*I went into my shell for a while*." I was immediately struck by the fact she was presenting to me with a thickened shell of skin and here she was using language to match. I invited further comment, and within the next 3 to 4 minutes she used the words "*I went into my shell*" 3 times. Moreover, she further volunteered in her description of being taken back to her home by a friendly gentleman: "*I went inside the four walls of my house, and closed the door, and sat and sat and sat*." In the few weeks following the injury skin thickening developed first in the legs and then became more generalized.

I sat listening to this, wondering what sense to make of it. I enquired about aspects of her life. She had enjoyed very good health throughout her life, but it seemed that the accident compromised (*"shattered"*) her sense of herself as perennially invulnerable. Moreover the embarrassing injuries to her face induced social withdrawal. She had actually started to improve by the time I saw her and the possibility existed that this was a response to the drugs she had been on. I enquired of her as to what she felt was the cause of her improvement. She related it to a friend who had come to her and said that she should get active again. She said that she improved again as she started to "*come out of my shell*." This "shell" theme was the metaphor she persisted with in both her language and her body.

I suggested to her that the thickening of the skin was a bodily (somatic) representation of what she was also expressing in using the term "shell." She accepted this, though without much insight. I encouraged her to continue to be active and resume her previous social contacts, and suggested I follow her up regularly for support, encouragement, explanation, education, and revision of her home situation so that coping could be ensured for as long as possible. After the third visit she declined further sessions. One year later both she and her physician reported marked clinical improvement, and she was on no medication.

***

The fall appears to 'shatter' this elderly woman. She reacts to this disintegrative experience by constructing a 'shell' around herself, and develops thickening of her skin. Her language, in her use of the word 'shell,' repeatedly expresses this motif. More than this, she expresses the same theme in the 'action' dimension of her life: she retreats inside the 'shell' of her house. Thereafter she does not improve until she dares to 'come out of my shell.'

How should we respond to this? The meanings data that emerges can hardly be dismissed as sheer coincidence. In the event I was startled, and then transfixed, by what I heard. It was one of those occasions when I develop "goose-bumps," faced with something both utterly intriguing, and which pushes my concepts beyond my comfort zone. And on this occasion it was not as if I went looking for this woman's 'story.' In a way the 'story' found me. The truth is that early in the consultation I had tried to brush aside her desire to tell me about the garden centre accident. I wanted to get on with the real (sic) history! For her part, she knew nothing about my mind/body interests, and indeed, later, she remained quite un-insightful about the meaning of her symptoms.

The strength of this somatic metaphor lies in the striking nature of the skin abnormality forming a thickened shell around Eunice, the vividness of the language she uses to state exactly how she felt and how she behaved, the mutual appropriateness of the language and bodily manifestation to each other, and the obviousness of these connections to an open-minded observer, who hardly needs to do any work at all to understand what has happened.

The second example of somatic metaphor is in some ways more complex:

***

Katrina, a woman in her twenties has struggled with massive obesity from age thirteen. Finally she conquers it by having a gastric bypass operation, losing some 60 kilograms in weight. At last the obesity is behind her. But the problems associated with her obesity appear in another form. She works as an acupuncturist. Since losing weight, and transcending her enormous weight problem, she has become more and more irritable with clients who seek her help for what she sees as relatively trivial bodily concerns. Compared to her struggle with obesity many of these clients have little to complain about. She no longer wants to tussle with 'bodies.' As this irritability increases she develops chronic nose and sinus catarrh, congestion, and infections resistant to antibiotics. She *can hardly bear to face'* some of these clients. Her nose may settle for a while when away from clients, but as soon as she leans over these troublesome clients demanding solutions to their 'trivial' problems her nose starts to pour fluid. They get *'up my nose.'*

***

Katrina's reaction to her clients, many of whom are, in her view, pre-occupied with relatively minor aspects of their appearance, is actually presented in *two* somatic metaphors. She tells me the story of her struggle with obesity, and of her growing impatience with her clients. She has difficulty 'facing' these clients, and develops increasing symptoms around the face. The first metaphor then has to do with 'facing.' But there is a second metaphor; these clients get 'up my nose.' When she leans over them her nose starts to pour. Her nose is much less of a problem when she has times away from client work.

The two metaphorical elements seen in Katrina's case raise some interesting issues. As a clinician, I participate in an extended dialogue with her that serves to uncover these meanings. The result is that I, the participating 'other,' become a party to the meaning-making. I am the person who nurtures a focus on meanings by the very questions I ask. There is a risk that I, with my meanings focus, could suggest meanings not intended by the patient, because I am determined to see meanings. Despite this possibility, I suggest that in Eunice's case a *strong* somatic metaphor exists because I was more or less forced by the encounter to see the connections. They burst into my awareness. In the case of Katrina, I had more a sense of searching for meaning, though in the end it just fell out, and was obvious to both of us.

My use of the term 'somatic metaphor,' as a labeling device for the form of meaning-*full* disease in which the language representations and bodily representations of meaning are remarkably congruent, is on closer examination somewhat problematic. There are two main reasons for this. The first is whether the conditions I am describing actually qualify to be regarded as metaphors. This may only be an issue for purists in the use of language. The second is whether by using the term somatic metaphor I am perpetuating a dualistic view of persons. These issues need to be addressed.

The word 'soma' is Greek for 'body.' 'Somatic' therefore means 'bodily,' or, *of the body*. The term 'metaphor' is used in the context of our human ability to symbolize. In using the term 'somatic metaphor' my only intention is to point to the fact that in many meaning-*full* diseases we see this capacity to symbolize in a bodily form, and in disease.

This intimacy between the body and our symbolic function is recognized in other academic arenas. For example, modern mind/body linguists such as Kovecses (2003), and Lakoff and Johnson (1999), argue that language has a metaphorical structure deeply rooted in bodily experience. In this view language is deeply *embodied*, it is not an activity emerging from a mind that is separated from the body. This is relevant to meaning-*full* disease. Let's explore this linguistic contribution a little further because it really does emphasize the closeness of body and language.

Kovecses points out that, strictly speaking, a metaphor 'bring(s) two distant domains (or concepts) into correspondence with each other. One of the domains is typically more physical or concrete than the other (which is thus more abstract). The correspondence is established for the purpose of understanding the more abstract in terms of the more concrete.' (Kovecses 2003, p. 4) Thus we have 'source' and 'target' domains. Examples of such pairings are 'boiling with anger' or 'burning with lust.' 'Boiling' and 'burning' are the more concrete *source* domains, and 'anger' and 'lust' are the more abstract *target* domains. Though we know what is meant by these phrases there is no way boiling and burning are really part and parcel of anger or lust, except as a linguistic device, and, yet, 'the two different things that are formally identified are indeed *similar* in some very significant but highly implicit way' (Bohm and Peat 2000, pp. 32–33, italics original).

In the light of this we can ask the question whether Eunice's disorder is really a somatic metaphor? In the abstract mode of *language* Eunice repeatedly uses the word 'shell.' In the apparently very different mode of *bodily disease* she develops a physical 'shell.' So it does looks like we have a (somatic) metaphor, at least in a conventional Western perspective, which, in dividing mind, thought and language off from the body, makes mind and body two very different things or domains. In this view it might be said we are bringing the 'two distant domains (or concepts) into correspondence with each other' and therefore we do have a somatic metaphor.

But it is all more complicated than that. Kovecses comments below (Kovecses, personal communication) on Eunice's case, from an academic linguist's vantage point. To understand the comment we need to realize that his commentary is about whether my proposed somatic metaphors are *real metaphors* or not. He is speaking from a linguistic point of view. Readers should also keep in mind the concepts of source and target domains mentioned above. In the phrase 'boiling with anger' we understand the *target* domain 'anger' in terms of the *source* domain 'boiling.'

***

"I believe that the illnesses you mention may be metaphorical ill-nesses. If it is the case that you first have the notion or idea of retreating to your 'shell,' then the metaphorical source domain can be considered to be realized non-linguistically, i.e., in an embodied way. Actually, this is quite common in metaphorical concepts, but your cases are much more scary because the realiza-tion of a metaphorical source domain actually produces a phys-ical disease. Can we be sure that the notion of SHELL came first, and then the thickening of the skin? If yes, we have a 'material-ized' metaphorical source domain for SHAME as target. Or, just the opposite, did the thickening come first, followed by the notion of shell? If yes, the patient unconsciously found an appro-priate (matching) metaphorical source domain (SHELL) for the target of THICKENED SKIN. In the first case, we have A PER-SON IN SHAME IS A SHELL, while in the second we have THE THICKENED SKIN OF A PERSON IS A SHELL. Both are metaphors, of course, but the second case is much less interest-ing. The first case would be shocking because the source domains we (unconsciously) think can be dangerous, in that they can turn into physical-bodily reality." (emphases in original)

***

It is not the main issue here, but one can immediately see the prob-lems we get into when we divide Eunice up into a more bodily aspect (her skin manifestation) and a more subjective aspect (her language use of 'shell'). She becomes a composite, constructed of source and target domains in accord with the linguistic concept of metaphor. Then we end up having to decide which came first, in a linear causal way. It is obviously reasonable to divide 'boiling with anger' into two domains. *It may be less appropriate to divide mind and body, and language and disease, into such separate domains.*

It can be seen that the disadvantage of the label 'somatic metaphor' is that in a certain way it does perpetuate the mind/body division. But, paradoxically, it is also very useful because it emphasizes the *bringing together* of meaning and disease, mind and body. Therefore, I use it merely as a useful communication device for the latter purpose. Having said that I admit we really do need to move beyond the concept of metaphor because, as we will see, the categories of meaning and disease should be seen as emerging from a unitary reality, rather than being construed as some strange conjunction of subjective meaning and dead matter. And, as a matter of fact, the linguists are going in a similar direction.

Kovecses (2003) and Lakoff and Johnson (1999) challenge, from linguistic and philosophical vantage points, the prevalent notion that we have a separated, independent, disembodied reasoning mind. As I said earlier, they argue that our thinking and language has a deeply metaphorical structure, which takes its shape from the way our physical bodies interact with the environment from the earliest moments of our existence. Our physical experience, mediated through our sensory structures, plays a huge part in structuring our forms of language. For instance, Kovecses says that the early experience of feeling warm, while being held affectionately, leads ultimately to the commonplace metaphorical language 'they greeted me warmly' (Kovecses 2003, p. 50) The point is that the metaphorical structures of language, thought, and communication arise eventually out of such embodied experience; they are rooted in the physical experience of the body, bodily function, and bodily activity. Language and meaning are thus deeply rooted in the body.

This linguistic evidence for the 'embodiment' of language is best understood by examining practical examples, and a summary of Kovecses' observations on anger is pertinent. Anger has a 'feel' to it, but when we describe it we resort to metaphors, such as 'full of rage' and 'boiling with anger.' Let's look at the metaphors underlying such statements (Kovecses 2003, pp. 21–3, 142–146, adapted). The first metaphor involves two concepts: Anger as a substance and anger as a container, or more accurately anger is a substance in a container (*he was full of rage, try and get your anger out of your system, she is boiling with anger*). The container metaphor is extremely useful because it captures intensity (*filled with*), control (*contain*), loss of control (*could not contain it any longer, boiling over, exploding, bursting with anger*), and dangerousness (*exploding*).

Kovecses (2000, Chapters 8–9) further points out that the fundamental metaphor of *anger is a substance in a container* exists in English, Hungarian, and Chinese, languages of very different origins. The metaphor has also acquired specific cultural variations. In English (an Indo-European language) anger is a hot fluid in a container (you make my blood boil, why don't you simmer down?). The same 'hot' metaphor is seen in Hungarian, a Finnish-Ugrian language of very different origins. But it is different in Chinese. The Chinese notion of 'excess *qi*' for anger causes pressure in the container, leading to explosions, but it is not hot. In Japanese, the anger is indeed hot, and in a container, and is largely conceptualized in the stomach (anger boils the bottom of my stomach), and, as it gets out of control it rises up through the chest, finally reaching the head whereupon it can no longer be contained.

All of these diverse cultures and languages conceptualise anger as a pressurized container. Why is this so? The argument of Kovecses, and of Lakoff and Johnson, is that they do so because in all cultures the peoples experience their bodies, bodily change, and bodily activity, such as urination, defecation, and bleeding as emphasizing the container structure of reality, giving rise to the container metaphor. The early experience of the body structures the shape of language.

Language, concepts and meanings are therefore seen, by these modern linguists and embodiment philosophers, as at least partly structured in the format of the body. In a measure, we are seeing here the return of the body to the mind, an example of the emerging notion of *embodiment*, which we shall return to later. Examination of linguistic metaphors shows us that even when we attempt to isolate language as a mental and linguistic activity the body is truly and deeply present. The point is over and over again that body and metaphor, body and language, body and meaning are all deeply interpenetrative. The fundamental dividing of body and language, body and meaning, body and subjectivity is increasingly untenable.

A term like somatic metaphor may be seen as fatally flawed in that it retains an element of mind/body separateness. But in my use of it here I am drawing attention to the way these apparently different domains actually come together, in the conjunction of meaning and the diseased body. Whatever we may say about the appropriateness of the term, the main point is that that form of the body we know as the *diseased body* can also no longer be divided off from meaning and language. And somatic metaphors, if we can legitimately use that term, are the most vivid representation of the conjunction between symbolic meaning and bodily disease.

CHAPTER FOUR

Language-making and disease

Somatic metaphors raise many questions as to the *nature* of *personhood*, and whether, within the Western cultural and scientific traditions, we have got an adequate framework for understanding persons and their diseases. Because we actually discover somatic metaphors through the *correlations* of the manifestations of *physical diseases* with *patients' meanings* conveyed through *speech* and *language*, an exploration of *language-making* in relation to meaning-*full* disease is crucial to an examination of the nature of personhood. Let's begin with a short story:

***

A woman, aged thirty four, complains of eight years of nasal congestion, facial soreness, and puffy eyes, all beginning when her mother was diagnosed with scleroderma, a very serious disease that causes both skin and internal organ damage. I could not find an allergic cause for the daughter's symptoms. Discussing her mother, the woman says: "I will always grieve."

***

A key element of this rather simple story is the congruence between the daughter's long-standing physical symptoms of tears, congested nose, and puffy eyes, and her language of grief. I see this sort of congruence every day in my clinic, if I listen carefully to my patients. The connections appear so self-evident that we might wonder why anyone would question them. But things are not that easy. If, having discerned congruence of mind and body manifestations in the patient's presentation, I go on to openly formulate an understanding of the patient's disease as emerging within and because of the patient's languaged story, some patients will become unsettled, even very upset. Even though we can say that it is *their* language that prompted me to make the connections, my *underscoring* of those connections may not be at all welcome.

Thus, as we ponder the relationships between language, experience and physical illness, two main topics arise. The first is that the person who uses the language that leads me to meaning may in fact resist knowing that meaning. The second is that the way we language things influences how we imagine the relationships between our minds and our bodies.

The resistance of people to meaning-*full* disease has many roots, though I think the two most important are individual needs to deny painful emotional feelings, and Western culture-wide faulty thinking, which entrenches the separation of bodily experience from subjectivity and language.

The resistance of patients to the role of story is clearly seen in the dynamics of the doctor/patient consultation. When I point to a meaning, some patients imagine that I am suggesting that the illness is not so much in the body as in the mind. Certainly I *am* indicating that their stories are making a contribution to their illnesses along with other factors. But, as already mentioned in chapter one, this is frequently seen in a very negative light, reflected in patient statements, such as: 'so, are you saying it's all in my mind?'; 'do you think I am making it all up'; 'do you think I am a hypochondriac because you can't find anything seriously wrong in the tests'; 'do you think it's all in my head'; or 'you think I am not really ill and should pull myself together.'

There are two major issues here. The first is that the illness is conceived as either *all* in the body, or *all* in the mind. The second is that if the illness is all in the mind then there is a negative reflection on the patient.

The idea that the disease is either wholly physical or wholly orig-inates in the mind (must be psychosomatic) is very widespread in Western culture. It also has many roots, one of which is the way we manage our subjective experience and communicate it to others. This is a complex subject that has to do with the nature of language. The processes of thinking and speaking require us to divide the world up into *this* feature or *that* feature, to name them *separately*, and to then *choose between them*. Even simple conversations always include a path chosen and other paths not chosen.

There is in all of this an *either/or* structuring of the world (as con-ceived) in the minds and language of humans. So we have a wide-spread human habit of dividing many aspects of life. It is not a big step from dividing to polarizing these aspects. We divide mind off from body. We then polarize them, making them entirely different. Mind and body are constructed in our minds as different *entities* or different *compartments*. But we have actually imposed this structure of separation upon ourselves and others. As a result we can talk of mind and body as separate when in fact they may not be.

There is another element, a reductionistic tendency that most of us over-indulge. In our desire for control, mastery, simplicity, cer-tainty, or just plain tidiness of thinking we often attribute a phenom-enon *entirely* to one entity or the other. For instance, we like to blame one person for some bad event rather than see it as a more complex matter, as an outcome of many convergent factors. In matters of ill-ness such simplistic, reductionistic thinking can lead us to the view that a disease or sickness must be *all* in the body or *all* in the mind.

Finally, we commonly take this polarizing logic a step further and add good and bad to the mix. We view illness that (supposedly) emerges from the body as respectable or legitimate, and illness that (again supposedly) emerges from the mind as a reflection of weak-ness or madness. Carrying the good/bad aspect a little further we might then decide that the patient is blameworthy for doing some-thing illness-inducing to him/herself.

Thus, the reductionistic processes that we impose upon reality include the following steps or options:

- the division of aspects of the whole into categories
- the reification of such categories into entities or compart-ments

- the forcing of phenomena into one of these compartments or the other
- the attribution of positive value to one compartment or entity and negative value to the other

Putting this another way—if people are fundamentally 'wholes,' then in some sense, in these reductionistic processes, we violate the wholes by carving them up, structuring them in unnatural ways, reducing their complexity, and putting negative value on some important aspect of the whole.

If, then, patients are 'trained' to accept these reductionistic processes as truly reflecting the nature of their personal reality, it is not hard to see why it can be very difficult for them to accept a formulation of their illness as including disease/story connections, even if they do not have the added disadvantage that doctors have of being steeped in the assumptions of the biomedical model.

Let's now turn from resistance, based in patient's faulty assumptions and fears, to the role the processes of human thought and language has in actually promoting these problematic dividing perspectives.

It should be fairly clear already that I believe that the notion of *a* body that exists as a separate entity, and *a* mind that exists as a separate entity is fundamentally flawed. Albert Shalom (1985) in his very interesting book *The Body/Mind Conceptual Framework and the Problem of Personal Identity* addresses this by drawing attention to the profound shifts in emphasis that occur when we use certain linguistic modes, especially in relation to the verbs 'to have' and 'to be.' Obviously the verb 'to have' implies ownership and this is the crucial issue. For example, notice the shift in emphasis that occurs when we use these two verbs in referring on the one hand to our bodies or physicality, or on the other hand to our minds, subjectivity awareness, consciousness, spirituality, or sense of self:

> 'I HAVE a body' *versus* 'I AM physical' or 'I AM embodied'
> 'I HAVE a mind' *versus* 'I AM subjective' or 'I AM thinking'
> 'I HAVE an unconscious' *versus* 'Some of my experience is unconscious'
> 'I HAVE a spirit' *versus* 'I AM spiritual'
> 'I HAVE a self' *versus* 'I AM me'

The use of *I HAVE* rather than *I AM* makes the point clearly. The *I HAVE* language makes me the *possessor* of a *thing* called the body or the mind. *I* become an owner of this *thing*, the body or the mind. Note also that the *I* and the *thing* (that the *I* has) become separated. In this use of language the physical and subjective aspects of our existence or personhood are made into several things or entities, and thereafter they are deemed to be separate in some way, to have their own separate existence. Owning things is a normal part of life, but how valid is it to separate the owner *(I)* from the thing (body, mind) in the case of the dimensions of personhood? As a way of speaking it is clearly very useful. As a reflection of the real nature of persons it may be very misleading.

The *I AM* usage takes us in quite a different direction. When I say *I am physical* or *I am subjective* or *I am conscious* the tendency to divide these aspects of our functioning into separate compartments seems to disappear. The *I AM* usage emphasizes the fact that I am an existing being, and that this state of being has various interpenetrating utterly integrated qualities: Physicality, subjectivity, spirituality, relational capacity, and a sense of self. We divide them into these categories or qualities because we want to think about them and talk to one another about them. We experience ourselves as enjoying these qualities. I know I am *physical* and *subjective* –these are aspects of my unitary reality, rather like saying water is both *wet* and *cold*. We cannot divide the wetness and coldness of water into compartments, they go together. We are dealing with different descriptors of the dimensions of experience in the same one entity (person in one case and water in the other). The I AM usage does not push me so much towards a division of subjectivity and physicality, or towards mind and body being different *things*.

I believe then that persons are better seen as an *I am* with bodily, mental, subjective, spiritual, and conscious (and unconscious) dimensions to our functioning, rather than as an entity made up of the joining together of relatively separate entities of body, mind, soul, spirit, consciousness or whatever people want to include as important components of human reality.

Let's pause and summarize where we have got to so far. Our starting point was the congruence between physical disease presentation and the patient's language. Then, beginning with the phenomenon of resistance to becoming aware of this, we explored the tendency we have to separate and reduce things, and indeed, to believe the mind/body whole is fundamentally made up of separate parts and entities. We have also seen that such separating is in the nature of language-making, but that some forms of language increase and others decrease this tendency, which suggests we need to be careful as to how we speak of mind/body realities. At a very real level we 'construct' them as separate realities.

I want to return to the linguists again for a moment. I referred in chapter three to Lakoff and Johnson (1999) who, in *Philosophy of the Flesh. The Embodied Mind and its Challenge to Western Thought*, and from a linguistic structural perspective, contest the prevalent notion that we have a separated, independent, and disembodied reasoning mind. We recall the argument, that our thinking and language has a deeply metaphorical structure that gradually takes its shape from the way our physical bodies interact with the environment from the earliest moments of our existence. Our physical experience, mediated through our sensory structures, plays a huge part in structuring our forms of language. The early experience of feeling warm while being held affectionately leads ultimately to the commonplace metaphorical language 'they greeted me warmly' (ibid p. 50). The point is that language, thought, and communication eventually arise out of such embodied experience; they are rooted in *physical experience*.

In some sense then the early holistic and very physical and subjective, but verbal language-*free*, experiences of the infant are fundamental, and remain fundamental for all of us however mature and adult. Verbal language and thought are subsequent differentiated products built on such experiences in beings who have the potential for, and who, over time, develop the capabilities of conscious self-reflection and language.

Lakoff and Johnson (ibid p. 48) argue that before these capabilities are developed by the growing human child there is a period of *conflation*. We can consider the infant in the first few months of life as experiencing life as some sort of preverbal holistic integrated structural unity where *subjectivity and physicality are indivisible*, or conflated. The infant has a multitude of experiences in which sensory and motor experiences are not only simultaneous with, but are also fused (conflated) with subjective experience and feeling. They are experienced as a *gestalt*. No parent doubts that his/her six weeks' old infant with 'colic' is experiencing a vivid mix of physical and subjective distress. Such parents are hardly likely to wonder what is going on in the infant's mind *as opposed to her* body though they may yearn to understand and meet the need. The physical and the subjective are interpenetrating aspects of one multidimensional whole.

As we grow and develop as infants we begin to differentiate and sort these aspects and categorize them. We actually address ourselves to the task of dividing up our experience, dividing up the 'wholes' into parts. This dividing and categorizing is a most useful function, especially for communication with others about aspects of the whole, and for manipulation of aspects of the whole. It is also very useful to begin to distinguish between myself and mother, and mother and others. In fact, part of development is to learn to divide the world up in the ways all other beings in our culture have divided them up. In another culture we may learn to divide them up rather differently, but that is another issue.

An important question is when is dividing a good thing and when is it not? This brings us back to matters of the body and the mind. While it makes reasonable sense to divide myself off from mother is it so sensible to divide mind off from body? The answer may be in the affirmative, if we are talking about communicating with others about our physicality and subjectivity as different issues for us. The answer is clearly the opposite if, in so doing, we set in train a process that excludes personal meaning from consideration in our diseases. The question then in relation to mind/body separateness is this: are we actually, *as languaged beings*, now dealing with things that are truly separate, or, are we really only dealing with language-based conceptualizations of *aspects* of the 'whole' as *parts*?

I mentioned previously that one of the operations of language is to actually choose one aspect of the whole against another aspect. We take a pathway through the whole, choosing one aspect after another, which means in effect that we are choosing against other aspects. At every point in language-making I am deciding towards one thing, and therefore deciding against a host of other things. Language rests on differentiation, categorization, and choice. I am always selecting out an aspect of the world as a way of communicating about it. Thus language induces separateness, or the separating of things.

Returning now to the infant and its holistic gestalt nature, we might consider that we did not in fact lose that fundamental holistic nature when we developed language. What we developed over time was a capacity to symbolize things in language form, to use language in self-conscious reflection, and to divide many things, which are essentially indivisible, into categories, so that we can think of them and communicate about them. *The person as a whole did not become truly separated into body and mind, but language created conditions whereby we could conceive of them as separate.*

The separation of mind and body is at some level an artifact or by-product of human language-based handling of human experience which is nevertheless fundamentally unified.

But it is not only the person that gets divided or 'constructed' through language-making. Lakoff and Johnson (ibid p19-20) make the further point that our experience of *external* reality, the world (not just the body and the mind), is also carved up into certain categories because we have the peculiar types of sensory perception (vision etc.) that we have. The way we are 'wired' for sensation and perception allows us to let in certain sensory signals and not others. Most of us tend to think we are seeing reality as it really is, but in fact we are seeing it in a very selective and restricted way. Bats and dogs see, hear, and smell the world very differently.

We have then this tendency and capacity to carve up and shape reality, to *construct* our realities, or to impose our human *narratives* upon reality. It gets more complicated. Not all constructions are inevitable. Some constructive elements are clearly negotiable, and I refer to ways of seeing or dividing things that are not due to the way we are 'wired,' nor due to the nature of language-making, but are more related to ways in which certain cultures have skewed thinking down a certain path. For example, many commentators assert that Western culture, after Descartes, has clearly followed a path of increasing separation of mind and body, a path that had many useful sequelae but was unfortunate in the light of the way we have ended up excluding human subjectivity from having a role in disease.

In summary, I am saying that the language of the patient, and the patient's experience in the body, of disease, are not really as separate as they might appear. We can construct them as separate, and if we ignore the story part that is exactly what we are doing. The question then becomes—what happens when we look at a patient's disease as if they are not separate? Let's return to the story of the patient Eunice, the woman with the thick skin described in the previous chapter, and look very closely at the various phenomena that emphasize the multidimensional unity of the person. Risking repetition to make this important point, I will give an abbreviated version of the story, emphasizing the three different dimensions in which she expresses herself: *physically* in the form of skin thickening; *in language* when she says 'shattering' and 'I went into my shell'; and *in action* by isolating herself inside her house.

***

Eunice has generalized thickening of the skin, and tissues under the skin, causing uncomfortable splinting of the chest, and tightness of the arms and upper legs ... She startled me by saying that it began when she fell over in the local garden nursery, sustaining injuries to her face and legs ... She described the fall as *"shattering."* ... I asked what effect this event had had on her. She replied: *"I went into my shell for a while."* I was immediately struck by the fact she was presenting to me with a thickened shell of skin and here she was using language to match. I invited further comment, and within the next 3 to 4 minutes she used the words *"I went into my shell"* three times. She was taken back to her home by a friendly gentleman: *"I went inside the four walls of my house, and closed the door, and sat and sat and sat."* In the few weeks following the injury skin thickening developed first in the legs and then became more generalized ... She had actually started to improve by the time I saw her ... She said that she improved again as she started to *"come out of my shell."*

***

The most obvious way to interpret this is as follows. Eunice has a personal experience, a fall, which has very significant meaning. We quickly ascertain its meaning *for her* from her language. It was *'shattering.'* We conclude, from other things she says, that the basis for this shattered response has been her relative good health, and very few challenging events in her life allowing her to put off coming to terms with the fact that life tends to deliver up some jolting setbacks, her growing awareness of her vulnerability as she ages, and her shock when her underlying fears of such things happening are ultimately realized by falling. 'Shattered' is a good summary word for her. Her long-standing (but eroding) view of herself and the world is well past its 'use-by-date.' She is tipped into the real world. We have little difficulty in understanding her reaction in an emotional and metaphorical sense. She withdraws *'into my shell,'* to protect herself. But it is more than emotional and metaphorical, it is also physical. She even creates a 'shell' in the form of thickened skin, and she makes use of the shell provided by the walls of her home. Eunice's personal meaning is pervasive—we can see it in every aspect of her dimensions of expression. In whatever she does she expresses this meaning.

If we were accustomed to 'reading' bodies as well as we read peoples' words, we might have come to the conclusion earlier in the course of her illness that the fall had indeed greatly affected Eunice, and said to ourselves something like this: *'Eunice has thickened skin, and she has 'holed up' in her house and will not come out, and it all followed the fall. She is protecting herself, strengthening her 'walls.' I wonder why that fall was so important to her'?*

My conclusions can be stated simply. Firstly, the meaning pervades her personhood. Whatever way we look at her we see it. It comes out as naturally in her body as in her language or her actions. The same meaning is communicated in every dimension—that is, using the symbols of words, or body function and structure, or action.

Secondly, I see no reason why I *must* ask the either/or question—did the experience occur first in her mind or her body? The experience is in her 'totality,' it is there in her physicality and in her subjectivity at one and the same time. Of course we can, and indeed do, impose a time sequence on the data. We could say that she was predisposed to being shattered by the long experience of 'good luck' throughout her life. She was triggered into this problem by the fall, so certain physical events came first. Then she constructed (in her mind) a way of looking at it that included being 'shattered,' and a need to withdraw and protect herself. She then, by some mysterious means, converted those notions into a bodily shell and into a retreat behind the walls of her house. This is one *narrative* of the events, a narrative based on a mixture of notions including time sequence and cause/effect linearities, and mind/body separateness. This is definitely one way of formulating the scenario, but its great weakness is, as we will see, that it gets stuck around how a separate mind with all these interesting meanings (of being 'shattered' and needing a 'shell') can convert them into such vividly specific disease phenomena. An alternative narrative is that she is an holistic being who has the capacity to express this distress (occurring in the whole) simultaneously in a variety of dimensions of her functioning, and that is what we are actually seeing.

Thirdly, the expression in Eunice's body seems as 'natural' as her expression in words. The words and the bodily manifestations both tell the story in their own way and both tell it eloquently.

Now let's bring in the contrasting *I have* and *I am* language presented earlier. Clearly Eunice had an experience that involved her whole person, not merely her mind, nor merely her body. We could say the experience involved the *I am* that has physicality and subjectivity. The experience is full of meaning and this is demonstrable in every dimension. Of course it could be that it might be most prominently expressed in one dimension or another and we will address that later. But it can be seen that the *I am* construction makes it easy to see how meaning flows in all dimensions.

In contrast, the *I have* construction of compartments of body and mind implies the origin of meaning in the mind as opposed to the body, and it follows that we then have to tackle what turns out to be the impossible task of tracing the passage of meaning from the separated-off mind, to the brain, and then to the body to manifest as thickened skin. There are two hurdles to be overcome. The first is that we must solve the mind/brain problem. The second is that, assuming we have solved the mind/brain problem, we must then solve how body systems such as the nervous, endocrine, and immune systems can create such exquisite somatic metaphors as illustrated by Eunice. We will confront these issues in detail in the next chapter.

We have been focusing on disease as a powerful manifestation of meaning, particularly in relation to language-making. We are long used to the notion of 'body language,' but can we go as far as a notion of 'disease language'? Is it possible that the physical body can represent 'experience' and meaning for us, whether we have the capacity for language or not? Pursuing these lines of thought requires us to consider some of the categories or dimensions of personal experience and expression that exist in their own right, independent of language, even though we often use language to represent them in our communications with others. I am thinking particularly of feelings and emotions and of our fundamental capacity for experience.

The subjective meanings that we have been discussing in Eunice's story have been those of being 'shattered,' of needing a 'shell,' of retreat (into a shell), and of the need to protect one's self. It is obvious that all of these have both a conceptual and a feeling quality. The 'shattered' and 'shell' words imply more than just an analytical description of structural breakdown or reinforcement. Intuitively we know that they indicate the presence of one or more of a variety of possible feeling-states including perhaps fear, dread, or bewilderment, to mention just a few. The meanings we find in meaning-*full* disease are highly associated with such feeling-states, so let's turn to feelings as an important aspect of meaning-*full* disease.

The language used to define feeling-states is often confusing. Taylor et al. (1997) have attempted to clarify the confusion and a direct quotation underscores the experiential and conceptual complexity that besets this important arena:

***

While the word *feeling* refers to the subjective, cognitive-experiential domain of emotion response systems, and the word *emotion* refers to the neurophysiogical and motor-expressive domains, *affects* are composite states encompassing all three domains. ... as well as mental representations of feeling states intertwined with memories of experiences that give personal meaning to current feeling states ...

***

It would be an over-simplification, but we can say that *feelings* are a label often used for the conscious subjective aspect of feeling-states which are close to language, whereas *emotions* are a label for the bodily subjective aspects of feeling-states. And again, roughly speaking, *affects* are a label for feelings and emotions combined. I suspect that in dividing up aspects of emotional functioning into these categories we have divided that which ultimately should not be divided, except as a means for discourse, in the same way that mind and body should not be divided.

But these categories do have some utility. We can start with the notion of *feelings*. Feelings are our *conscious* subjective experience of states like sadness, fear, anger, joy, hope, love and so on. But people vary in their capacity to label their feelings, and I frequently work with people who are good at recognizing some feelings and not others. At times it is clear that something very important is happening in our persons, and yet we do not actually know what we are feeling. Matthis (2000) speaks of "'feeling-like' sensations of movements within ourselves that we can neither name accurately as this or that specific feeling, nor rationally discard as not being a feeling." These states are *emotions*. The clues as to their true nature are inferred from how we feel in our bodies, or discern from observing and considering our behaviors. She argues that emotions are experienced subjectively, but are more bodily in nature than are our feelings. Faced with an angry patient I might feel my body tense up, my heart race, and my voice tighten. The occasion is certainly full of emotion, but afterward, on reflection, I might have difficulty saying exactly what the feelings were.

The third category, *affect*, on the other hand, is

***

the generalized concept for all those embodied processes that, when they reach consciousness, can be perceived on the one hand as feelings and on the other as emotionally charged physical concomitants. These may be perceived as, for example, burning in the skin, a racing heart or shortness of breath: Bodily signs that we readily interpret as the expression of an emotion. [Matthis 2000]

***

Affect is then the more general label for that state of being that may be expressed in subjective feeling, or in bodily emotion, or both. It *includes* feelings and emotions. Affect and its dimensions are crucial to meanings, and evidence is growing that disturbance in affect *regulation* is a key element in the development of disease states (Schore 1994, Taylor, Bagby, & Parker 1997, Carroll 2005). So we might say that affect and meaning are the closest of companions.

Pausing again for a moment, let's reflect on what we are doing here. It is hard to erase the impression that in whatever way we categorize these states we are still left with a more basic whole. In fact, the more I start to define them the more I start to wonder at the legitimacy of dividing them up. All three categories seem to be aspects of one another. The term *feeling* stresses the subjective aspect, the term *emotion* the physical aspect, and the term *affect* the fact that they seem part of one unitary experience. These categories of feeling, emotion, and affect all reflect aspects of personal expression. The separateness of the categories is primarily in our *language*. I am using language to divide up the affect/emotion/feeling-laden *experience* of persons. In the case of *feelings* this experience reaches clear consciousness in a form that may be verbalized in the symbolic mode of language. In the case of *emotions* there are bodily elements that we experience, and which we are conscious of.

Sometimes this affect-laden experience is expressed or experienced only in the body. Matthis gives an illustrative example of this. We can look sad, and behave in a way suggesting that we are operating out of an experience of sadness, and yet when asked what our feelings are we can be totally unaware that sadness is a central driving force in our behavior. Thus, this affect/emotion/feelings *territory* is rooted in an underlying 'affective matrix' giving rise to mental processes (feelings) and biological processes (emotions). Matthis has called this underlying level of experience the 'basic processes,' reflecting the impression we have that there is beneath all our categories a unified holistic substrate.

Let's now return to Eunice. At a 'basic processes' level she has a core reaction to trauma, which we surmise (using our languaged understanding of human experience) triggers a destabilization of her world, a threat to her sense of survival, a state of bewilderment because the world is no longer coherent in terms of her experience, and raises the possibility of fragmentation. This disturbance is expressed in both mental processes ("I was shattered," "I went into my shell") and biological processes (she develops a thickened skin).

Again we can see that in all this we are carving Eunice's experience up into aspects. That is what human consciousness does with everything. Such activities are 'dependent ... on consciousness: that agency ... which makes the pretentious claim to being the guarantee of truth, but is merely the bearer of discontinuous reflections of something else that lies beyond it' (Matthis 2000). Of course this same 'carving up' tendency will then tempt some to try to divide the 'basic processes' level further by asking such questions as—are the 'basic processes' fundamentally physical or fundamentally subjective? For me the conclusion is that they are neither, they are in fact both, and inextricably together. This takes us into a later chapter where we will examine the possibility that 'experience' is fundamental.

In summary, we are beings that experience, and who become beings who can project that experience into the form of symbolic verbal language and thought. We certainly experience powerful emotions, even when we do not have the capacity to project them into thought or verbal forms (as in early life). At times there appears to be no really vivid or obvious representation of meanings in our conscious thoughts, even though we may unconsciously reveal them in the way we speak. Frequently we do not recognize our emotions in clear consciousness, or express them clearly in language, even if we have the capacity to do so. In fact, often we just express them in bodily form. We see this, for example, in the many bodily changes that occur instantly in the face of a threat to survival, and also in many cases of meaning-*full* disease.

CHAPTER FIVE

Meaning-*full* disease explorers

The assumptions of biomedicine dominate the provision of healthcare in the Western world. These assumptions can be summarized fairly succinctly without much risk of contention. The body is a biological 'machine.' Body and mind are separate entities; although there is a connection between them, it is appropriate to consider the body as separate to the mind, and it is appropriate to deliver healthcare by focusing solely on the body. 'Real' disease will usually be adequately and completely explained by physical mechanisms; thus, mind, soul, or spirit aspects are peripheral or even irrelevant. Disease occurs in an individual's 'machine-body'; thus, disease is more or less an individual's bad luck and/or responsibility. These, then, are the basic assumptions, and they have many consequences. For instance, concepts of relationship, family, cultural, societal or other non-physical forces causing individual illness are hard for clinicians to integrate into their thinking. And the so-called 'psychosomatic' illnesses must be seen as a special and separate category because for most physical illnesses there is no really relevant role for the mind.

But there have been many voices clamoring for a different perspective. Harold Kaplan (1980, pp. 1843–1853) in a lucid essay titled the *History of Psychosomatic Medicine*, has drawn attention to the many psychoanalysts, psychiatrists, physicians, physiologists, and psychologists who have, in the 20th century, attempted to formulate enduring models for the way human disease is affected by human subjective experience. Risking invidious comparison we can point to important early figures such as Sigmund Freud, Georg Groddeck, Sandor Ferenczi, Franz Alexander, Harold Wolff, George Engel, and Zbigniew Lipowski, but there are many others. There has been a huge amount of research and writing on topics such as stress and disease, psychological factors and immunity, personality styles and proneness to disease, emotion in its bodily aspects, and the notion of psychosomatic illness.

Despite all this activity there have been only a few who have recognized strong connections between highly specific meanings and disease. I have reservations about some of the ideas and emphases of this small group, but an examination of their writings allows me to underscore the typical ways in which thinking develops in people who recognize meaning-*full* disease. It also draws attention to the risks of *meanings fundamentalism*, by which I mean an excessive application of meaning to all diseases, and the tendency to ascribe highly specific and stereotypical meanings to each disease.

I will begin with Georg Groddeck (1866–1934), a pioneer for meaning-*full* disease in a very unsympathetic era. Groddeck wrote extensively about the meaning of illness. My attention was drawn to him long after I started discerning meanings in the physical illnesses of my patients. As mentioned in chapter one, I experienced belated reassurance in discovering that this German physician, from a very different age and intellectual climate, had also seen many instances of somatic metaphor, and that, apparently, his meanings-based approach resulted in many remarkable recoveries of chronic physical disorders. Early influences upon him included Bismarck's personal physician, Schweninger, who favoured diet, hydrotherapy, and massage over therapy with drugs. Later, Groddeck and Sigmund Freud engaged in a lively correspondence extending over many years. Freud seems to have been very impressed with Groddeck, though saw him as being on the margins of psychoanalytic orthodoxy. Groddeck's writings (see Schact 1977) are studded with clinical stories, many of which are similar to those I tell in this present book, except Groddeck gives them a psychoanalytic coloration consistent with his relationship with Freud and the psy-choanalytic ethos of his time and work.

In chapter one I described one of Groddeck's cases (Groddeck 1928), a man with retinal (eye) haemorrhages originating in a trau-matic incident to do with a crucifix, and readers may care to remind themselves of the details. What we see in that case is the same exqui-site matching of meanings and physical manifestation that I have observed in my work. More than that, a realization that these phe-nomena could not be contained within conventional medical mod-els of disease drove Groddeck, as they do me, to try to develop an adequate explanatory theory. The result for Groddeck was a central explanatory concept of the 'It.' In his first letter to Freud he says 'the distinction between body and mind is only verbal and not essential ... body and mind are one unit ... they contain an It, a force that lives us while we believe we are living' (Groddeck, in Schact 1977, p. 9). In the concept of an 'It' he seemed to be stretching for a unified and unifying unknowable depth beneath the surface of things, a sur-face which we persist in dividing up into categories such as mind, body, soul, and spirit. The It was 'the great mystery of the world' (Groddeck, in Schact 1977, p. 11) or even the 'God nature' (ibid). Groddeck's 'It' actually has little appeal for me, partly because the term itself, at least in English, carries a rather cold objectifying qual-ity. 'It' seems to imply a 'thing,' and, not only that, it is a 'thing' somewhat separate from other functioning aspects of me. Thus, Groddeck's language implies a dualistic separation between the It and myself. But I can see that he was, in his own way, trying to cap-ture an aspect of being that is prior to, and gives rise to, all the known categories of physicality and subjectivity, and for that direc-tion in his thinking I have considerable sympathy.

Perhaps more radically, and relevant to the ways in which meaning might permeate disease, Groddeck believed the It, as *essential being*, had an inherent ability to symbolize. 'Groddeck con-siders man's compulsion to symbolize to be an expression of the It and not of conscious thought' (Schact 1977, p. 17). He believed that from our earliest beginnings we are symbolic creatures. 'Because we think and feel symbolically, we are, in short, tied to the symbol as to something belonging to human life, it is possible to look at everything in human existence symbolically' (Groddeck in Schact 1977, p. 7)

In this view, the symbolic function stretches across the whole of reality including of course the body and its diseases. This is a radical idea, and I accept that many would regard it as bizarre, but, once one accepts the phenomena of meaning-*full* disease, the search for an explanatory model definitely raises this possibility. We will expand this theme in other chapters, but the argument goes like this: If we accept that adults often have meaning-*full* diseases; and, if we accept that the lives of adults are in an unbroken continuum with the lives of fetuses and infants; then, is it really acceptable to imagine that meaning only penetrates disease once certain conditions are fulfilled? These conditions would likely be that meaning-*full* disease can only develop once the infant has developed a capacity for language and symbolization, and the ability to absorb symbolic meaning from the family and cultural discourses in which we are bathed from birth. This limited non-essentialist and post-modern view (see below) requires an explanatory theory for how meaning can pervade disease sufficient to create, for example, a somatic metaphor. In contrast, Groddeck's view, which allows meaning-*full* disease from our earliest beginnings, must explain what the symbolic function really represents when it provokes meaning-*full* disease in an infant.

There is a further issue. If it is unacceptable to posit a discontinuity between immature non-languaged humans and more mature languaged humans, then it is perhaps unacceptable to posit such a discontinuity between humans and other species. This leads to the even more bizarre possibility that animals have meaning-*full* diseases. At this point of course the very word *meaning* itself comes under scrutiny, as to whether it is the best term for what we are trying to grasp. Again, more on this later, when we address the subject of *experience*.

In the Groddeckian model, in our pre-verbal lives as infants we are symbolizing creatures, raising the possibility that without verbal conduits for symbolizing meaning the infant may use the conduit of the body. From a meaning-*full* disease perspective adults with sophisticated language function frequently express unutterable and unconscious emotional and meanings intensities in the form of bodily disease. Does that imply a symbolic function outside language?

Groddeck's propositions are what most moderns would call 'essentialist' in the sense they propose something more 'essential,' the It, beneath or behind the surface of human functioning, human perception, and human construction. Such a notion would, of course, be regarded as not only quaintly old-fashioned and modernist but also entirely erroneous by many post-structural thinkers who eschew any notions of 'essential' forces behind the surface of things. The idea that a symbolizing meaning-making something may exist as an essential prior to family, language, and cultural discourse is contrary to much current thinking. For Groddeck this mysterious something, the It, unifies the 'parts' of persons, the parts we call mind, and body. The question arises as to why his thinking went towards the It? The key lies in realizing that for Groddeck, the 'body and mind are one unit.' I think there were a variety of significant contextual elements that shaped his conceptualization of the It, but it seems to me that people who observe meaning-*full* disease, and who begin to contemplate the implications, do all drift towards a unitary view of the person, an essentialist perspective (which in this post-modern age is not that fashionable), and, ultimately, to a more spiritual construction of life.

Many decades later we can, of course, draw on many new scientific resources that were unavailable to Groddeck, and which enable us to develop a comprehension of meaning-*full* disease through the twin notions of the underlying unitary connectedness of things and that the whole is deeply represented in its parts. Let's pursue the latter idea a little further.

Groddeck, looking backwards and in a literary direction, called on Goethe saying:

***

(Goethe) who showed science a new approach, namely, the approach of seeing the part in the whole, of taking the apparent whole as a symbol of the universe, of seeing the whole world symbolized in a flower, an animal, a pebble, the human eye, the sun; and to construct the world from this flower, this pebble, that is to create it anew and to investigate things not by analyzing but by placing them in the context of the whole. [Groddeck in Schact 1977, p. 252.]

***

We have access to more modern versions of this idea, for instance Pribram's holographic paradigm where, in the words of Wilber (1985, p. 2):

***

The part is in the whole and the whole is in each part—a type of unity-in-diversity and diversity-in-unity. The key point is simply that the part has access to the whole.

***

We will develop this idea further, but we can see that Groddeck, in this respect, was well in advance of very modern thinkers as he grappled with the tensions between matter and meaning, raised by the observed clinical phenomena of meaning-*full* disease. He was clearly reaching for a view of reality that allows the whole and the part, the mind and the body, intimacy and separateness, and the disease and its meaning, all to be seen in each other.

Groddeck also clearly saw disease as a *communication*. Groddeck posited the It as a governing core reality within the person, a force which expressed in the language of the body certain needs, directions, and issues for resolution. In a remarkable sentence, which cannot have endeared him to many, he says:

***

In the first place – I claim the validity of this sentence for all illnesses, every form of illness and at any age – the meaning of illness is the warning "do not continue living as you intend to do." [Groddeck in Schact 1977, p. 199]

***

Disease is, for Groddeck, definitely a communication, and more specifically a *warning*. The shoemaker's retinal haemorrhages were a sign, a symbolic system, a demand by the shoemaker's It to resolve his guilty feelings with respect to the destroyed crucifix. When these were uncovered, confronted, and attended to, his eyes settled. We can infer several things from this construction. The It seems to be a more knowing and deeper aspect of the person. At times the It appears to be the voice for the things we want to avoid. At other times the It seems to have the real power, and our lives are determined by this powerful fundamental, communicating, warning, force within. Indeed, Groddeck's It seemed to 'live' the individual.

While we do not need to adopt these constructions in their entirety they do emphasize some aspects of meaning-*full* disease.

Disease does break through. It does tell a story. Listening to the mes-
sages of our illnesses has a certain urgency. Illness is not just an
unfortunate turn of events in a vulnerable biomedical 'machine.' It
may indeed be that, but it may also be a vivid representation of
something very meaningful and very important to deal with if one
is to become well again.

Though Groddeck was highly regarded by Freud his influence
faded. It seems that psychoanalytic and psychiatric thought, as it
developed through the twentieth century, could not accommodate
the close relationships between disease and human subjectivity
implied by somatic metaphors, with their intertwining of powerful
symbolic meanings and the body. The dominant models of science
and medicine with their mechanistic views of matter and biology,
and the traditional separation of mind and body, made his work
strongly counter-current. His close relationship with psychoanalysis
would not have helped, as psychiatry and many of the new psy-
chotherapies threw off the constraints of psychoanalytic doctrine
and modes of practice. Moreover a growing emphasis on theories of
'stress,' the connections between the nervous system and the
immune and the endocrine systems, the emergence of systems theory
and its emphasis upon the multidimensional and multifactorial
nature of things, the modernist disavowal of anything metaphysical,
and a host of other forces, left notions of highly meaning-*full* disease,
at least in the sense of somatic metaphor, pretty well dead and
buried. There were, of course, many notable contributions to the
field of psychosomatic medicine, which do not come into the
province of this book.

We now turn from Groddeck to the more modern psychoanalytic
emphasis of Luis Chiozza and colleagues, in Buenos Aires. Chiozza
has been publishing in Spanish on meaning-*full* disease and somatic
metaphors since 1963, but, recently, two books have appeared in
English (Chiozza 1998a, 1998b). As far as I can see, Chiozza's work
has been largely ignored in the English medical and psychotherapeutic literature. There are fairly obvious reasons for this. Apart
from the fact that meaning-*full* disease was itself fairly unacceptable
to the dominant therapeutic discourses of the twentieth century
there is also the issue of inaccessibility to non-Spanish readers. But
there are other elements in Chiozza's approach that may have
weighed against wider acceptance.

I became aware of his writings in 1999 after they appeared in English, and, as with Groddeck, I was struck by the similarity of our clinical experiences of patients with very 'organic' or physical diseases showing startling symbolic elements. Chiozza and his colleagues present numerous detailed examples of a variety of physical conditions, but I will refer only to his views on the meaning of psoriasis.

Psoriasis is a disfiguring condition of the skin of unknown cause, though genetic factors do play a role. My experience in treating this condition is limited, but our group has treated several patients with severe psoriasis all of whom were referred to us after many years of symptoms, and having received all available treatments with minimal effect. We have gone on to use mind/body-oriented psychotherapy and have had some excellent outcomes. Because it is risky to generalize from a few cases I had developed only tentative ideas as to what psoriasis might represent in a meanings sense. In chapter one I have already cited the case of Emily whose psoriasis cleared when she dealt with her boundaries, attractiveness, sensitivity, and autonomy issues. These seemed to be the relevant themes driving her illness. Her severe disfiguring and chronic psoriasis of seventeen years standing resolved with psychotherapy, and remained almost completely quiescent. Whatever statistics-oriented clinicians may say about single case research design, surely this case points to something important.

With that introduction we turn to the perspectives of Chiozza and his colleagues on psoriasis (Chiozza 1998a). They draw heavily on Freud's ideas, at times quite impenetrably. A lot of their discussion seems to pivot around how their views actually fit into Freud's original thinking, and how they are managing to enlarge that thinking. This preoccupation with Freud and Freudian theory may be one reason they have not been particularly influential. But they do see meaning-*full* disease and have grappled deeply with the implications.

I will briefly summarize Chiozza and colleagues' understanding of psoriasis. The skin is a 'contact surface' and a 'barrier' against stimuli. It defines the body and is intimately related to the feeling of identity. Touch helps us define ourselves (by touching our own bodies), and ourselves in relation to other persons (by them touching our bodies and us touching theirs). The skin is an organ that both touches and feels. It forms a container.

Remember the issues of my psoriasis patient: She wrestled with not being sufficiently boundaried, and being forced into someone else's 'mould'; and she is too easily 'touched' by other people's feelings; and so on. We might also recall Kovecses' emphasis (Kovecses 2003) upon the body as a container, giving rise to language that is full of container metaphors (*full* of rage, *bursting* with pride, etc.). Of course Kovecses, as a linguist, tends to see the body as coming *first*; after all language is preceded by body. In this view the container quality of the body gives rise to 'container'-based language. There is really no suggestion of the reverse possibility of meaning shaping the body. In fact, as we saw in chapter three, Kovecses considers such an idea to be 'really scary.'

Chiozza's position is rather different. He does not think of body shaping mind, or of mind shaping body in linear causal ways. He thinks of physical and subjective elements as being in there together, rather than one leading to the other. An example of this is where he puts two words together that we normally would keep well apart. He says we have a 'skin-ego.' In this usage he is intimating the closeness of body and subjectivity to the point that they really are one. He says:

***

When we consider an individual's skin as a "wrapper," insulating and differentiating the person from his or her surroundings, we assume that the skin is the limit: everything external is the "world" and everything that remains inside is the "ego" ... The feeling of lack of protection that accompanies situations in which the ego is insufficient as a container leads to defensive reactions that may take the form of hardness and inflexibility in the areas of behavior or character ... They may be expressed in the skin as, for example, a hyperkeratosis. The patches of hyperkeratosis express the fantasy that they function like the shell of insects, which as invertebrates, lack an internal skeleton but develop an external structure that provides them with both protection and support. [Chiozza 1998, p. 14]

***

This quotation emphasizes the scope of Chiozza's conceptualization. Firstly, the subject's feeling of lack of protection, and the function of the skin as a barrier, are brought together into the same conceptual space. In this view the skin is the *bodily* representation of the *felt* barrier between the experiencing organism and the external world. The skin is not merely a necessary 'coating' on a biological mechanism. Of course it *is* such a coating. It is also the physical representation of our experience of ourselves as having a boundary between our inner world and the outer world. Secondly, when that boundary is challenged or threatened in some way, the skin naturally represents the organism's response to the challenge or threat. Changes in the skin are to be expected. Thirdly, some of the skin's options, when the organism is under threat, are a throwback to earlier patterns in our evolutionary history. For example, psoriasis is seen by Chiozza as a scaly change in the skin representing an attempt by the organism to retrieve some of the boundary protection achieved by insects with their hard external skeleton.

Kovecses' view, based in his discipline of linguistics, inclines to the materialistic concept of the physical body as a major structuring influence upon language and meaning. In our physical body we are a container, therefore our thoughts, ideas, and language are pervaded with container metaphors. Chiozza's view, on the other hand, inclines more to the view that we *are* a *subject body* (he does not actually use that term, which I will address in chapter ten), and when we are threatened in our subject-body-selves we represent that in our physical bodies in the form of diseases. There is a causal element in which the direction seems to be from subjective experience to our physical being, from the subjective experience of threat (or lack of protection) to a bodily skin representation of psoriasis.

There is some justification for Kovecses' model because we are able to discern a certain amount of linear causal patterning in our experience, and because there do seem to be structuring effects of body on mind and language. In contrast, Chiozza reaches towards a model in which the organism is both physical and subjective, in the same time-space, and in which the skin is a natural and automatic site for these meaningful experiences to be manifested, as demonstrated in the condition of psoriasis.

While some of Chiozza's concepts will be seen by non-psychoanalysts as rather old-fashioned or regressive in their adherence to many aspects of Freudian theory, and in their preoccupation with how they vary from Freud's views, there are aspects in which he is very forward- thinking. This comes out, for instance, in his discussion of the two epistemologies (or bases for knowing).

***

'In the first epistemology, body and soul as well as time and space are different ontological realities existing beyond consciousness. Nature is sharply differentiated from culture, and the psychical world is formed, *from* matter and *in* living matter, when such matter acquires sufficient organization to include a nervous system or some type of "brain." ... In this theoretical framework, knowing is nearly the same as knowing the cause and being able to explain the mechanism that causes an effect. The other epistemology holds that body and soul as well as space and time are *notions*, categories established by consciousness to describe a reality that is in itself incomprehensible. In this epistemology, in which "body" is what is perceived by the senses and "psyche" is what possesses meaning, the myth acquires proximity to the object of knowledge. ...' [Chiozza 1998a, p. viii, italics in original]

***

Essentially, what Chiozza is saying here is that there is a core unified reality, which can only be known via our consciousness, which structures it in certain ways. Our sensory perception and our language-making divide our experience into categories. In recent centuries our systems of knowledge and categorization have strongly emphasized the separateness of body and mind dimensions. This is the *first epistemology*, which creates an excessively linear causal sequencing in which we must decide whether body or mind come first. But the *second epistemology* holds that these separated categories lie 'above' an unknowable territory: 'Both myth and science are different maps of an inaccessible territory.' (Chiozza 1998a, p. viii) Put another way disease and meaning are different representations of the same core reality. Here we are then, back to something similar to Groddeck's own body and mind as one unit, and a unitary reality beneath the appearances of separateness.

One of the problems with Chiozza's approach is its tendency towards 'essentialisation.' Faced with a somatic metaphor such as

Emily's psoriasis, with its obvious and florid connections between meaning and disease, it is all too tempting to generalize excessively. For example, one of my earliest patients with a chronic facial rash talked about 'keeping a brave face' on her husband's depression. We addressed this, and the rash resolved. But this does not give us license to see 'brave face' issues in everybody with a facial rash. While I do think there are common patterns I am careful to avoid excessive generalization.

In Chiozza's writings it is frequently difficult to discern whether the clinical story or meanings material provided in relation to an individual patient is a direct transcription of *actual statements* made by the patient, or whether we are getting an interpreted version in the words of the clinician. While I think Chiozza's group have courageously pursued meaning-*full* disease and have much to teach us, I also think they have developed overly firm ideas as to exactly what this or that physical disease manifestation means. The risk of this tendency is that the patient ends up being squeezed into the clinician's pre-determined system of what individual diseases *must* mean. This is a problem that we have quite enough of in the modern practice of biomedicine with its denial of meanings and insistence that disease is purely physico-material in its origins. If we return to Emily's psoriasis we see that there are themes relating to boundaries, interpersonal sensitivity, attractiveness, and autonomy. While it is legitimate to store such insights it is not legitimate to assume that the meanings aspects of the psoriasis of the next patient I see can automatically be reduced to these conceptualizations. There may be things in common but there will always be individual differences and emphases. One has to go to the patient and listen very carefully to discover the exact meanings material relevant in this or that case. A patient I am seeing as I write this chapter underscores the importance of listening to the exact talk of a patient rather than coming to the patient with preconceived notions of what must be the case:

***

A woman aged 33 was referred for assessment of multiple symptoms including an odd 'tingling' sensation on both sides of her head, a worsening of her previously mild allergic nose and throat symptoms, and an aching at the back of her neck. She had seen three general practitioners, an Ear, Nose, and Throat specialist, and had had CT scans of the head and neck, and nothing had been found except for some minor allergic thickening of linings of her sinuses, which could hardly explain her tingling or neck symptoms, but which was compatible with her worsened nose and throat symptoms. When asked what her tingling felt like she said "it's like a cloud over my head." She also said that the symptoms consistently disappeared when she did one of three things: When she lay down, or put her sun-glasses on, or donned her sun hat. These details mystified me. The timing of the onset of her symptoms was explored. They came on one month after returning from a holiday in the tropics, and about the time she stopped her anti-malarial medication (which she was inclined to blame for the problem). Still unsure where I was going, I asked her about her life in general and her holiday and discovered that she worked in a boring, menial, but 'safe' job, felt chronically under-achieved, and that the holiday in the tropics represented a temporary escape into freedom, spontaneity, and exploration. Coming home reversed all that. Suddenly I realized that the lying down, the sun-glasses, and the sun hat symbolically represented freedom, spontaneity, and exploration. The cessation of the anti-malarial medication was the breaking of the final link with the holiday. Home-life was stifling, and the local climate hardly tropical; suddenly the phrase a 'cloud over my head,' and the physical symptoms, became eminently understandable.

***

If we attempted to approach this woman's symptoms via the concept of 'stress' we would not get very far. While there is a sense in which we could assess her as stressed, it is too general a concept to get at the real underlying meaning which needs to be recognized before she can understand that her need to break out of her life 'cage' has become so urgent that her body is expressing it symbolically and very unpleasantly. Nor is it reasonable that from now on I should approach all patients with sore necks, worsening allergic eye/nose symptoms, and curious sensory symptoms of the scalp as having the same issues as she does. That is meanings reductionism.

A tendency to *meanings reductionism* is found in an extreme form in the work of the populist self-help author Louise Hay. Many years ago, in an odd circumstance, again well after I was established in my own explorations of meaning-*full* disease, my (then) young son found Hay's book *Heal your Body* (1982) lying on the driveway to my house. I can only assume someone felt I should read it! Hay has an interesting story. She describes herself as a 'teacher of healing,' who was raped at age five years and was 'a battered child.' In adulthood she was diagnosed with cancer of the vagina. She decided that this was a bodily representation of her childhood experience of rape. Against medical opinion she embarked on an active 'mental and physical cleansing,' and within six months was declared to be clear of the cancer.

As far as I can tell Hay's philosophy seems very similar to that of Groddeck. Symptoms are seen as an expression of something that is not right, essentially as a warning to 'not continue living as you intend to do.' But her book essentialises the meaning of every body structure and disease, and every disease is assigned a fairly limited and even glib meaning. Simple corns on the feet, for example, represent 'hardened areas of thought—stubborn holding on to the pain of the past.' But what about tight-fitting shoes? It is easy to become simplistic in relation to meaning of illness. In my own early thinking about psoriasis I had concluded that, if meanings were involved, then most likely they were around a sense of 'badness' that must not be seen. The 'badness' was then 'seen' in the bad, ugly skin condition of psoriasis. This conceptualization did not fit Emily (the patient described above) very accurately at all, though there was some sense of badness tied up with the other themes. But the barrier/ boundary issues, and the problems of sensitivity to the world and others, fitted very well, and working with these issues seemed to be associated with an otherwise totally unexpected improvement. The message is that while we should remain attuned to meanings, and will accumulate experience of the range of possible meanings, we must always go to the patient for the truth.

Louise Hay has a huge lay following, and there are few of my mindbody workshops where at least some participant has not heard of her or read her books. But I would caution against meanings *fundamentalism*. While it may be true that meanings are entwined with all our illnesses, it may not be the most important element, and the meaning may be very buried, and, indeed, not accessible at all. Secondly, I would caution against meanings *essentialism*. By that I mean we should avoid imputing simplistic stereotypical meanings to any particular condition. Life is far too complex for us to say all back pain means this, or all facial rashes mean that, or all brain tumors mean something else. The proper attitude is one of open enquiry to discover what meanings can be discerned in the individual patient's language and consciousness. There will be general patterns, but one must always begin with the reality of *this* particular person and patient, not with all the patients one has seen before. The easiest way to offend a patient is to fail to engage with their reality by projecting our assumptions, theories, and realities upon them.

Finally, I turn to the work of James and Melissa Griffith who have written an interesting and in many ways very helpful clinician-oriented book entitled *The Body Speaks: Therapeutic Dialogues for Mind-Body Problems* (Griffith and Griffith 1994) One of their emphases deserves discussion in the context of meaning-*full* disease and language. At the centre of their approach is a huge regard for language and the way we are shaped by stories. We are 'immersed' in a 'sea of language … from the moment of … birth' (ibid p. 30). They lean heavily on Heidegger who 'found the notion that people create language to be an absurd joke: People do not create language—they are created by language. In his words, "Language is the house of Being. Man dwells in this house" (ibid p. 30). This is, essentially, a post-modern position. In the end, what we have is the pairing of *matter* and *narrative*. All meanings have to do with the stories and language we are born into, in which we are immersed from birth, or perhaps conception.

The Griffiths have a model of disease that focuses upon 'unspeakable dilemmas,' which in the end must be expressed in the form of body symptoms. And certainly this is a modeling I use constantly in my work. Their clarification of the issues of therapy around this model is highly informative. But, if one looks through their book, they include no examples of what are traditionally called 'organic' diseases—diseases that show substantial measurable physical abnormalities in the tissues. Their focus is upon somatoform disorders, or that general grouping of disorders seen as 'functional' or 'psychosomatic.' For example, they focus on headaches and 'pseudoseizures,' but not other neurological disorders like multiple sclerosis. Why is this so? If they are so interested in 'story' how is it that they either don't see stories in the 'organic' disorders, or perhaps don't tell those stories (which I think very unlikely)? I believe it is because they are working out of post-modern assumptions, so that they end up with a way of working that implicitly or explicitly includes the following: Matter is fundamental; language is secondary, though from the earliest moment we are immersed in the sea of language and 'story'; the body speaks through 'psychosomatic' disorders when the person cannot find another way of expressing unspeakable dilemmas; and we do not consider the 'organic' disorders because they are rooted in the fundamental 'matter' where language and meaning do not penetrate, and which is somewhat separate. They are therefore still operating out of a fundamental mind-body dualism which does not allow us to see meaning-*fullness* in the 'organic' diseases. But many examples of *somatic metaphor* require a model of persons that allows meaning-*fullness* in many disorders where there are obvious measurable changes in the tissues of the body.

CHAPTER SIX

Disease as communication

A t times, the *matching* of meanings and disease is so vivid that the disease appears to be *communicating* the meaning. In chapter three I presented the stories of Eunice and Katrina as examples of somatic metaphor. In Eunice's case we saw the direct communicative impact upon me, as the observing clinician, of the symbolic image of 'shell' in both Eunice's language and her body. The potential for the communication of meanings increases because of the manifestations in both the linguistic and the physical dimensions. This leads us to consider disease as a form of communication.

Within the context of physicomaterialist Western biomedicine such an idea must be considered bizarre. But I will risk derision and seriously consider the issue, because the category we call *meaning* is so closely linked to the symbol-making categories of *thought, language,* and *communication* that a discussion of disease *as* communication becomes an inevitable aspect of a wider discussion of meaning-*full* disease.

We have already seen that Groddeck saw disease as a communication in a rather special way, as a deeper aspect of the individual (the It) speaking to a more conscious aspect of the same individual. In this view disease is a kind of built-in warning system for an individual who is otherwise not confronting an important reality that needs resolution. Certainly, when I see patients with physical symptoms rooted in unacknowledged or unresolved issues, one of the ways of helping patients make sense of what is happening is to conceptualize the symptom as a representation of a part of them calling attention to something that needs attention. Here is an example:

***

A 59 year old man was born with a paralytic condition of his legs. As an infant aged 5 he lost his mother suddenly, and he was subsequently reared by a close relative. He adapted well to life and indeed enjoyed a balanced, fruitful existence, and a happy marriage. There appeared to be few consequences emanating from this difficult start. Certainly his legs were a problem and, as he put it, 'my wife was my legs and I was her voice.' He acknowledged that he had got through his life 'depending upon my strong arms.' This was interesting because he presented to me with a history of several years of itchy band-like hives of the hands and forearms *but on no other parts of the body.* When I explored this further I discovered that the problem began in the context of the deaths of the close relative who had 'mothered' him and of one of his 'sisters' (one of the children in the adoptive family). This had been very upsetting for him. He felt 'abandoned' and 'despair.' It became clear that the deaths had awakened the issues of loss in childhood. But there was more. Over the years he had developed a personality style that required him to be strong, resilient, and emotionally non-disclosing. But, gradually, as he got older, and his wife was less strong, the equilibrium they had developed together was showing signs of disintegrating. They were not able to maintain their garden in the same way. They were not as able to be as available for their children as they had expected. So the losses of people important to him echoed the losses of childhood, and the erosion of the defensive resilience the couple had achieved together, combined to stir up a core issue of vulnerability. His arms, that were his strength and symbolized a compensatory resilience, developed a problematic rash that undermined his ability to use his arms, and therefore undermined his abilities and strength at a literal and a symbolic level.

***

The message is clear, but who is talking to whom? Is it a message from him to himself? Is it a message to important people in his world who have learned to expect him to be forever strong and resilient, a tower of strength for them? Is it a message to his spouse that the equilibrium must change as life goes on and strength inevitably wanes? Is it a message that must come out but only in the code of physical symptoms? Is it a warning (as Groddeck and Hay would posit) that here is something to be resolved, and, if it isn't, there may be serious consequences?

The notion of disease as communication, if we accept it at all, is actually a very complicated matter. For example, if illnesses are pervaded with meaning, then inevitably they will be pervaded with issues of interpersonal relationship, because most of our meanings arise in the context of such relationships. Our discussion of disease as communication involves exploration of other categories such as experience, meaning, thought, language, and interpersonal relationship, all of which are interdependent. It is similar to the issue of thinking about mind and body as separate categories when they are not really divided at all.

Returning to Eunice and Katrina we have, firstly, Eunice, whose thick skin is a startling physical representation of her need for a 'shell.' From a communications point of view it seems very clear and obvious. Then we have the acupuncturist, Katrina, who communicates her impatience with her clients in a physically vivid way. She has trouble facing these clients and gets symptoms in her face.

Katrina's nose symptoms represent the clients who irritate and frustrate her, just as dust and fumes can get up a nose and irritate it. The nose is a very reactive organ susceptible to physical irritants, and it may therefore be a natural conduit for physical symbolism in expressing emotional reactivity. The symbolic connections between the nose and frustration or anger have long been recognized in our cultural idiom, exemplified in our use of the phrase "he gets up my nose."

Because I did not get enough time, in the consultation with Katrina, to explore all the nuances of her physical manifestations, I may be missing other possible symbolism. For example, the nose and sinuses are organs for tears, and these symptoms could also represent tears of frustration. But without evidence originating in the patient's actual language I have no justification for imposing that possibility upon her presentation. I mentioned in chapter five the dangers of stereotyping the meaning of symptoms.

Implicit in the idea of communication is the fact of a *recipient* for the communication, a recipient who is able and willing to recognize or accept the meaning. As a clinician with a patient I end up being the recipient, but it is unlikely, if there is a more fundamental communications element to disease, that people develop diseases primarily to 'talk' with physicians. It is much more likely that I enable a patient's illness to become accessible through my ability to be with the patient in a listening and relational mode. The illness may, of course, have a prior communications value relating to or originating in the dynamics of the patient's family and close relationships. As a listening clinician I enter those dynamics and deploy my listening and relational capacities, and in effect become a *new* element in the communications dynamic.

Notice that I say that Katrina's body (face/nose) is *carrying* and *communicating* meaning. Is it right to go so far? It could be that the body is just *carrying* the meaning in a physically symbolic way. This raises the issue of the ultimate meaning of symbols. Groddeck asserts that the symbolic function exists from the beginning—that we are symbolizing creatures in our essence. Post-structural theory would argue that symbolism is always imposed, always secondary. We will return to such issues, but it is unquestionable that symbols carry meaning and meanings have little communication value unless they are recognized, either by one's self or by another.

In the case of Eunice we have 'shells,' 'four walls' and a 'thick skin.' Recognition of the symbolic here is not a problem for me— these are very concrete visual symbols and easily recognizable, partly because of the reinforcement achieved by the same meaning being expressed in several different ways.

But in Katrina's case I need a little more sophistication—the notion of 'getting up her nose' as an expression of frustration involves an implicit recognition that irritants do get up people's noses literally. That really isn't a problem because from childhood we all experience this phenomenon literally. Then there is the culturally conditioned usage of metaphor. 'He gets up my nose' might actually be confined to a culture or language; as we have seen from Kovecses' work, some metaphors are universal, others are not. We have therefore a very complex situation in which meaning and disease are mediated through common experience of our gross physical structure (myself as a walled-off container), common experience of the behaviour of organs (sneezing and catarrh from dust getting up one's nose), the symbolic structure of language (the way we bring two domains together to make metaphors—for example, a *person* getting up my nose), the conventions and discourses peculiar to one culture or another, and so on.

Put very simply though, I can search for meanings in her presentation because in English we do talk in certain ways together. But we can see that it is not just a simple (sic) matter of symptoms carrying meanings. It is also a matter of the meaning of meaning, and a matter of meanings being communicated (or more often not) between humans who have a similar cultural heritage.

Other questions arise. Is meaning inherent in a disease, whether the patient knows it or not, and whether the clinician picks it up or not; or is it somehow woven into the illness because of the culture we are immersed in, and we (the patient and the clinician) can both pick it up because we have that culture in common? I believe all these are true, though at different times and in certain circumstances one interpretation may seem more relevant than the others.

In a way, the issue we are tackling is the communicative intensity of a disease with meaning. It is important to note that I am not saying that all physical conditions with associated 'story' elements necessarily reach the communicative intensity of a somatic metaphor. The communicative intensity of any metaphor depends on two things. Firstly, it relies on how aptly and easily the two different categories or domains match one another. For example, having had a 'hugely exciting time' is well matched to 'whale,' at least in metaphorical terms, and often expressed in the phrase 'I had a whale of a time.' In Eunice's story the 'shell' language, the need for protection in the face of threat, and the thickened skin are all well-matched even though they are very different categories or domains.

Secondly, the strength or communicative intensity of a metaphor depends a great deal on the world of feelings and ideas shared by the patient and the clinician. There cannot be a somatic metaphor unless the patient's mind and body are deeply integrated. Equally there cannot be a communication with the clinician unless the metaphor emerges out of the patient's and the clinician's shared subjective world and their shared symbolic capacity.

This raises the interesting question of whether the illnesses *where we see no metaphorical element* are actually devoid of that element, or indeed of any meaning at all, or whether this apparent absence of meaning has more to do with my failure to discern meaning. That is, are we missing many meanings because we are not tuned into the communication aspect. Remember Groddeck's man with the deteriorating vision. Neither the man nor his previous physicians had been tuned into the meaning. Think of my patient, Eunice. Neither Eunice nor the physician who referred her to me considered the meaning of her 'shell.' Therefore the second element that influences the communicative intensity of somatic metaphor is the innate and acquired seeing and listening capacities of the observer/listener. The question is then how good are we at picking up meaning?

So far much of our emphasis has been upon meanings as discerned by carefully listening to *language*. But the reality is that experience and meaning are not ultimately dependent on language, though they are greatly enlarged by it. This issue is underscored when we consider meaning-*full* disease in infants, and, as way of entering this extremely challenging territory, let's return to the story of Jane, introduced in chapter one, who had lost all her hair (alopecia).

Jane was conceived, and gestated, in an ethos of dread originating in the stillbirth of an older brother. In infancy she showed numerous signs of anxiety relating to separation from her parents. Later, when aged three, she was separated from father, mother, and primary care-giver, more or less at the same time, and hair loss ensued. Subsequently hair re-growth and further loss seemed to reflect how things were for her, in terms of separation from her care-givers. We need now to focus upon the concept of *experience* before we can discuss Jane's case in more detail.

New-born infants cannot talk but they certainly do have *experiences*, even though we might find it hard to discern the exact nature of those experiences. In fact, as parents, we frequently struggle to know what is really going on with them. But whether we understand them or not they are definitely *experiencing*, a fact that is given far too little consideration, at least in biomedical circles.

Some infants gestate for nine months in a context of uncertainty, fear, regret, or ambivalence. Others emerge too early and endure long periods in incubators. Others are extracted by force. Some have anxious, ambivalent, or depressed mothers, who may struggle with breast-feeding. Many parents do not know how to relate intimately. Infants traverse the first few months of their lives without a verbal language to tell us what we need to know. Many of us are not acutely attuned to their non-verbal communications. How does an infant negotiate all this? In their reactions to the diverse experiences outlined above, what options of expression does the infant have?

For me it is no surprise that many infants develop somatic symptoms. I think that these infants are frequently communicating their *experience* through the body, or in the body. If we were to see their somatic expressions as meaning-*full*, how might it alter our responsiveness to them? Of course we commonly say 'she is not an easy baby' or 'he is unsettled.' We diagnose 'colic' or 'reflux' and feel we are 'on to the problem,' when, maybe, all we have done is describe these symptoms or syndromes from a *physical* perspective. Undoubtedly these little bodies are communicating personal distress, but I doubt that such suffering is fully encompassed within a *purely* physical analysis.

As adults we tend to associate meanings with language, and for most situations that works well. But when we conflate meaning and language, or, putting it another way, make language the sole vehicle for meaning, we get into trouble. Language is presumably the most powerful sign system for experience and meaning. But 'experience' is *prior* to the capacity we eventually develop to overlay experience with thinking, symbolic images, metaphors, image manipulation in our 'heads,' and talking. While this is true, it remains that the early experiences of the infant are meaning-*full*; they signify something. Jesper Hoffmeyer in *Signs of Meaning in the Universe* (1993, p. 7) argues that 'we tend to overlook the fact that all plants and animals—all organisms, come to that—live, first and foremost, in a world of signification. Everything an organism senses signifies something to it: Food, flight, reproduction—or, for that matter, despair.' The world is a *semiosphere*, pervaded with signaling and signs.

Returning to Jane, I would say that Jane's hair loss signifies her 'experience' of loss. I suspect the roots of her hair loss lie in the parental experience of still-birth. The potentials for separation, loss, and death are implicit in all developing life, and may be more so for Jane, given the experience of her parents of the prior still-birth. From our earliest days all of us embark on a somewhat fraught but 'normal' journey of attachment and separation, intimacy and isolation. Experiences of loss are constantly negotiated and renegotiated. I wonder whether Jane's early colic and reflux were actually physical representations of such early negotiations. I certainly think that the loss of Jane's father, mother, and day-carer, all at the one time, had sufficient experiential impact to destabilize her, and cause hair loss, which, in the event, became a very visible sign of something seriously wrong in her life. It can hardly be denied that these losses were experience-*full* and meaning-*full*.

There is, in all of this, the notion of a crucial theme (or two, or three) developing over years, finally being expressed in disease. Meanings, as we adults know them, build up in our lives from infancy, layer upon interwoven layer. Every meaning we deal or struggle with in adult life is really the tip of an 'iceberg' of meanings. The most deeply immersed part of the iceberg is a metaphor for meanings or experiences generated in early life, perhaps including even wider planes of meaning such as those envisaged by Jungian archetypes and Sheldrake's morphic fields. An increasingly complex structure of meanings builds and builds until something happens that activates or topples the whole structure leading to an open manifestation in various possible dimensions of personal expression including disease. In Jane's case, I postulate that themes of potential separation, loss, and death build incrementally, but it takes the *experience* of loss of the three main carers to topple her, and the hair loss occurs.

This helps address the question that many patients ask their doctors: 'Why have I got sick now?' The doctor may resort to a non-answer, saying something like 'that's just what happens.' Another will mention 'stress,' and the patient will protest 'but I have been more stressed in the past and didn't get sick!' A meanings approach to disease, with its implicit 'iceberg' formation over time, certainly helps in many cases as illustrated in the following example:

***

A woman in her thirties has suffered with chronic headaches since age 21. Her story reveals that the headaches first began when her father died of cancer when she was age 13. At that time they lasted some months and then disappeared. At age 17 her first boyfriend unceremoniously jilted her and the headaches returned, again for some months. At age 21 she became pregnant, and the father deserted her, disappearing to Australia. The headaches resumed and continued for many years. It was obvious that a variety of day-to-day interpersonal experiences contained potent ingredients able to trigger her underlying feelings of loss, slight, betrayal, and abandonment, all rooted in her experience with these earlier important men. It was clear that the new day-to-day experiences were like fuel feeding a fire that had started smoldering at age 13, and again at 17, but became a prolonged conflagration from age 21.

*****

Returning to our iceberg metaphor, the ultimate betrayal, at age twenty one, was the event that really toppled the structure that had been gradually developing around this set of meanings to do with loss, slight, betrayal, and abandonment.

An obvious question is what does Jane's *hair loss*, itself, mean? To be honest, I do not have a clear sense of somatic *metaphor* in this case. That is, I am not convinced that her hair loss is so *exquisitely appropriate* to her fears and experiences of loss that it had to be manifested in the body in this way. Maybe I am not seeing something important in her story. I am familiar with the idiomatic phrase 'he is tearing his hair out,' and I *could* impose the meanings implied by that phrase on Jane's story, but it is not really necessary to force the fact of her hair loss to such levels of meaning. But, equally, it is hard to push aside the idea that, in her case, the hair loss is a *sign* for, or does signify at some level, her 'experience' of loss, or threat of loss. We do not have to decide whether hair loss is *always* a sign for this particular issue of loss. It may or may not be. As we saw in the woman with headache another very different symptom may be an equally powerful sign for loss. In fact diverse symptoms may represent loss as one meaning amongst a group of meanings. For example, in the story about the man with hives on his arms (vide supra) the loss of his mother and other important figures was very important, though perhaps overshadowed by the derived issues of strength and vulnerability.

Hair loss is a sign of Jane's experience around loss. But, if this is a sign, to whom is she signalling? A ship may hoist an ensign but without another party the ensign enjoys no *efficacy* as a sign.

Certainly Jane's parents and her doctors were not reading the signs. A sign, even the sign of hair loss, needs a reader of such signs. A symbol needs someone who is symbolically aware.

The history of my awareness of separation and loss issues in alopecia began some years ago when I saw a six year old boy who first lost his hair when he was shifted, at age two, from his family of origin to a foster home, into which he was later formally adopted. His hair grew back in, and there were no hair problems until the next major move or change occurred when he went to school at age five. This, of course, involved some separation from his adoptive parents. His hair promptly fell out again. I interpreted the problem, at that time, as reflecting his destabilization around attachment, or what in psychotherapy we call separation/individuation issues. He and the parents did a few sessions with a child therapist, and his hair grew in over the six weeks of the therapy. Building on that rather meagre experience of managing alopecia with psychotherapy, and also knowing that, as an immunologist, I had no easy medication answers for Jane and her parents, I looked for evidence of disturbances of attachment, and as a result uncovered the story of 'losses' as described above.

All this might suggest that we could approach our subject by replacing 'meaning' with the more fundamental category of 'experience.' Perhaps, instead of meaning-*full* disease, we might talk of *experience-full* disease. This idea that experience is actually *more fundamental* than meaning is an important one, and we will address it further in chapter twelve. But, for the moment, let's stay with the idea of disease as communication.

If I hear or see birds, dogs, dolphins, or monkeys communicating, their symbolic systems have very little intensity *for me*, at least as a communication, because I have little ability to decipher the complexity and intensity inherent to their system of communication. Nevertheless, I would be a fool to assume such intensity was absent. The same can be said for my comprehension of the meaning of a foreign human language. Put simply, attempts at communication may be occurring without me being aware of it. By analogy, what sorts of meanings may we be missing as we face distressed infants with their troublesome physical symptoms, or adults with their inflammatory skin, gut, or joint disorders of unknown cause where we never even think of exploring the 'story?'

In the normal course of life, the infant and its parents grapple together with the infant's inevitable separation and individuation. The infant's journey to adulthood is one of gradual achievement of independence. While such processes are deeply related to the *acquisition* of language, the issues of separation, individuation, loss and abandonment are experiences that *predate* language formation. In a semiotic universe we should expect signs when personal disarray occurs around such crucial matters, and where language is not possible we should expect non-language-based signs.

I could of course probably find separation/individuation issues in most families. Thus, finding an apparent connection between the separations from father, mother, and daycare 'mother,' and Jane's hair loss may be a coincidence, or it may not be. While I believe we would have to be excessively sceptical to rule out any possibility of such connections in Jane's case I do accept that there will be some who remain sceptical. I think we make our choices, and many of them are largely built on ideology. If we say that meanings cannot provoke disease in this way we will prefer the view that the relationship between hair loss and separation is merely coincidence, or must be coincidence. If on the other hand we believe that a person is unitary, and that biology and subjective experience are profoundly interwoven, then we may see the hair loss as a sign for her attachment distress and get excited and want to attend to her attachment needs and see what happens.

Thus far I have emphasized two kinds of meaning and communication in relation to disease. The first is communication at the level of somatic metaphor, where the person's disease and the person's language seem to be saying exactly the same thing. In the clearest somatic metaphors the meanings seem to be naturally, directly, vividly, and obviously represented in both the body and the patient's language. A good example of this is Eunice's thick skin, or 'shell' of protection, which seems utterly appropriate to her sense of vulnerability and threat. The communicative power lies in its congruence with every other way in which she communicates. But it has no communicative efficacy if the observing clinician or the patient herself cannot see or hear the meaning, however obvious it might be to others.

The second type of communication is exemplified by Jane's hair loss. It may or may not be a somatic metaphor, but as the observing clinician I am not confident that I can see an obvious somatic metaphor. I guess one could say that she lost her parents and day-care 'mother' and also lost her hair, but that feels like straining for a metaphor. But, I am confident her hair loss was her signification of attachment distress. Maybe her 'colic' and 'reflux' were earlier forms of the same issue. The hair loss may be a temporary sign of distress related to loss. She may move to other signs in other systems as she gets older. Again the sign only has meaning if there is an observer who can see the signs, and that observer will only see the signs if he/she has a world view that allows meaning and matter (disease) to be in the same 'space.'

At the very least it seems obvious that Jane *experienced* distress in relation to loss. Whether it is appropriate to frame this experience up in terms of our adult concepts of meaning is a moot point. David Griffin, in *Unsnarling the World-Knot. Consciousness, Freedom, and the Mind-Body Problem* (1996) argues that our earliest experience is actually sense-*reception* and not sense-*perception*. From our beginnings as a foetus and infant, 'experience' can be powerfully felt (sense reception) even if it does not have the elaborate cognitive constructions (sense perception) that we, as older human beings, create around it and which indeed, for us as adults, are parts of the experience. Griffin is accessing the more primitive pre-thought, pre-verbal component of experience that we probably all have in an ongoing way, but which is easiest to isolate (from thought and language) in the foetus and infant. I will return to Griffin in chapter twelve.

In this current chapter I am endeavoring to entwine two complex elements. The first is a conceptualization of possible ways in which certain meanings enter the field of the infant and develop into a particular theme for that person, as time goes by, and as the person is exposed to life's vicissitudes. The second is the way in which such experiences and themes become an interpersonal communication.

There is an obvious wider question already alluded to but not yet directly addressed. Are people who present with illnesses trying, at some level, to actually communicate through their bodies, or is it merely that we are unified organisms full of meaning-*full* experience, and, because we are embodied, the body automatically expresses such meanings? From this it might follow that meaning-*full* diseases do not arise out of a primary communicative intent. On the other hand, because body, meaning, relationship, language, and communication are all part of one 'whole' it is reasonable to expect the meanings of disease to be visible in the field of view. As we enter relationship with the patient such meanings can be acknowledged, as emerging within the intersubjective space. They constitute a potential healing opportunity for the meanings-oriented clinician, just as the physicality of the body offers an opportunity for the surgeon to remove a cancer growing on the skin.

We can emphasize this point by analysing somatic metaphors further. A somatic metaphor implies at least three elements: A meaning-making person who communicates meaning, a meaning from that person's life story presented in the body, and a potential respondent. A strong communications interpretation of the somatic metaphor might be that a patient with a skin rash or bowel problem is presenting in that way as the *only* way (at least at that point) he or she has of communicating the distress in the 'whole.' This is not a radical view if a person is actually seen as a unitary 'whole,' and in particular, a meaning-making 'whole,' and that the body is a natural and usual place for disturbance in the 'whole' to be presented. In that 'strong' view of communication there is some drive to 'reveal' and the only way to do this is through the body.

A 'weak' communications view is really rooted in the acceptance of the person as a unitary 'whole.' A disturbance in the meaning-making 'whole' will inevitably manifest physically in the body, and that body representation will be at some level a vehicle for meaning, sometimes so clear as to have the communicative intensity of a somatic metaphor. There may be no formal drive to communicate, but where we have two people in relationship the meanings are there to be discerned, and picking up on the meanings may be a way of beginning a healing response.

If we look at illness in these ways we do have a radical new basis for looking at healing processes. The notion of communicative intensity of disease is very useful clinically. But as I have pointed out any such communication of meaning in disease is useless if the 'recipient' of the communication does not have 'eyes to see or ears to hear,' whether that recipient is the parent of an infant, a spouse of friend, or a healthcare-provider. The patient may have a very active disease imbued with intense meanings but who is responding to the 'communication?'

This takes us back to the question of the 'recipient' and the lamentable reality that clinicians on the whole are deaf and blind to meaning-*full* disease. Why are we so reluctant to 'see' this reality, and unwilling to be the 'recipient' of a communication that turns out to provide the key to relief of suffering which is our fundamental intent as clinicians? Who sees meaning-*full* disease is the question addressed next.

CHAPTER SEVEN

Who 'sees' meaning-*full* disease?

The visibility of meaning-*full* disease is ultimately dependent on the paradigmatic assumptions of the observer, but beyond these more fundamental elements there are a multitude of influences steering us towards one model of illness or another. Ascertaining a relationship between meaning and illness assumes both a willingness to look for such relationships, and an ability to be with the patient in such a way that the meanings and disease correlations can be rendered visible.

Our question, '*Who 'sees' meaning-full disease?*,' will be considered in the context of the fact that the *general* idea that 'mind,' or better, human subjective experience, plays a role in health and disease is now commonplace, even if it enjoys only marginal consideration in medical school curricula, or in the health plans and budgets of Western nations.

Throughout the twentieth century hundreds of medical and non-medical researchers and writers have pointed to clinical phenomena and research studies supporting the effects of the brain or mind on both animal and human immune and endocrine systems as well as disease states. The evidence for these effects, and the general subject of *mind/body medicine*, has been discussed and argued in many different popular, scientific, and academic forums.

For example, it remains persistently fashionable to invoke the concept of 'stress' as a catch-all for the role of human subjectivity in disease. Despite the obvious relevance and usefulness of the concept of stress, I remain somewhat ambivalent about it. I know what it feels to be stressed or overloaded, and that when that occurs I am subject to symptoms of one sort or another. Therefore, 'stress' as an organizing concept does make very good sense for some aspects of my experience. The problem is that biomechanistic physicians latch onto stress fairly easily and automatically because it fits with their fundamental assumptions. They understand that 'machines' get stressed if driven too hard, and so they can talk about 'stress' affecting the mechanistic body, without engaging with other thorny aspects of subjectivity at a deeper level. The problem I have with stress is that the 'stress' of life involves far more than a notion of an overloaded 'machine.' Stress is rooted in deeply personal meanings, which explains why one person's stress is another person's stimulus. For me 'stress' is a 'suit-case' word: It carries a lot of 'stuff,' but we need to open it up and un-pack it to discover its 'contents.' Inevitably, this un-packing leads to a focus on personal meanings. But, certainly, the concept of stress has played its role in maintaining the importance of human subjectivity in illness development.

Twentieth century thinking about 'mind/body medicine' has involved concepts far beyond simple notions of 'stress,' and two conceptual frameworks have emerged that have proved very useful and enduring. The first originated with George Engel (1977) who proposed the *biopsychosocial model* (BPSM); the very name tells it all. It constituted a clarion call for understanding illness as *multifactorial* and *multidimensional*. And this call was heard by many doctors, especially family practitioners, to whom, in the continuity of primary medical care practice, the presuppositions of the BPSM were self-evident. People got sick because of the conjunction of multiple factors.

The second framework is that of *psychoneuroendocrinoimmunology* (PNEI), which now constitutes the model most favored by the modernist scientific tradition for incorporating the fact that human subjectivity does influence disease. The field of PNEI is constituted by the large body of formal research exploring the influence of subjective factors on the body by examining relationships between various psychological categories (including measures of stress) and nervous, immune, and endocrine system functions. That is, the PNEI scenario assumes that human subjectivity influences the body towards disease via the brain which then influences the endocrine, nervous, and immune systems. For many biomechanistic physicians it is tempting to see this PNEI approach as all that is needed, ultimately, to map the connections between mind and body, psyche and disease. Unfortunately this is not the case.

The importance and strength of the BPSM and PNEI is that they *do* capture aspects of mindbody integration. They stress, on the one hand, that we are pervasively physical, bodied, and embodied (see chapters 8–10), and that there are always going to be physical correlates of what is happening in our lives. On the other hand, they assert that what is happening in a physical sense is not the measure of everything.

The problem is that ultimately BPSM and PNEI rest upon assumptions that create a number of major conceptual difficulties that are not easily solved. The most notorious of these is what is commonly called "the mind/body problem." Quite simply the problem goes like this: The old *dualistic* views of mind and body assume that the mind is a separate thing or 'substance' from that of the brain and body; if that is the case, how can it interface with the brain, which is an entirely different substance? Most people accept that the mind/body problem, emerging as it does from dualistic assumptions, remains insoluble.

This mind/body problem is especially highlighted by meaning-*full* disease. Assuming that the meanings we talk about in these diseases arise in the field of the mind, we must ask how these meanings get transcribed backwards into brain substance and function. In other words, we must solve the mind/body problem. Then we must solve how the brain interacts with the endocrine and immune systems to transcribe that meaning onto the highly relevant organ of the body, like Emily's skin or the boot-maker's eye? The endocrine and immune systems certainly have capacity to carry certain types of information, but, as far as we can tell, not the capacities required to create symbolic meaning in the physical tissues. We need other models, and much of this book is about developing these.

The problems do not stop there. The old physico-materialistic views of matter would argue that meaning-*full* disease cannot occur because they imply causation in the wrong *direction*. The idea was that the general direction of biology is *bottom up*. Genes (at the bottom) give rise to everything else. At a higher level of organization this means that brain gives rise to mind, and mind gives rise to meaning. The traffic does not go the other way. Interpreted simply, this means that meaning-*full* diseases cannot occur because they appear to be the result of a *top-down* influence, involving a direction from meaning and mind to brain, and from there to body, via psychoneuroendocrinoimmunological influence (according to PNEI). In short, the direction is wrong and the transmission of meaning cannot happen anyway because of the mind/body problem. We clearly need different models to explain meaning-*full* disease.

There are some obvious places to begin. Maybe mind and body are not really different compartments or substances? That is certainly the stance in this book, and we need to see how that idea follows through into our understanding of health, wellness, illness and disease. Anyway, the axiom that the direction of things is essentially linear and bottom-up is clearly wrong. The case for *top-down* effects from mind/brain-to-body is now based on solid research evidence that genes actually change their expression under the influence of psychosocial stress (Rossi 2004), and that this is one cause of deterioration in certain disease states. In that case, those of us who are willing to accept the existence of meaning-*full* diseases, but have a yearning for a biomechanistic explanation, might feel a surge of hope. Maybe meaning-*full* disease is really due to psychosocial effects upon our regulatory genes. But this argument or logic is really only a variant of the PNEI argument, except that it involves a new twist, a new dimension, by including effects on genes as part of the process. Unfortunately, such latter-day acceptance of top-down influences, from a vague mind/brain complex to the body, does not solve the problem of meaning-*full* disease, whether it goes through genes or not. This is because it remains very difficult to see how, on current models of brain to body messaging, *via genes or not*, a specific organ is chosen to tell a highly symbolic story in such an obvious degree of specificity that we shake our heads in wonderment.

The foregoing will have, at the very least, emphasized for readers that despite the dominance of biomedicine there has been widespread interest in mind/body medicine throughout the twentieth century. But there has been relatively little work on meaning-*full* disease, even amongst those one would imagine would be most interested. By way of illustration, I can point to the 2001 issue of the journal Advances in Mind/Body Medicine, a journal dedicated to the role of mind and body connections in health and disease. In that particular issue of *Advances*, twenty well-known mind/body authors and researchers cited and discussed what they regarded as the most compelling evidence for mind-on-body effects in diseases of many kinds. Their selections are of considerable interest, and the issue provides quick access, not only to compelling evidence of mind/body effects and interventions, but also to a range of notable mind/body thinkers and researchers.

But the real reason I point to that issue of *Advances* is that none of these twenty commentators, many of whom are leaders in the mind/body medicine field, address the phenomenon of *somatic metaphor*; nor does the wider pool of research endeavor and publications they have drawn upon. This is extraordinary, because these are all enthusiastic protagonists for mind/body medicine and yet appear to be ignoring what is, I believe, our/their most persuasive phenomenon. The problem is, I think, that they are not *seeing* the phenomenon. One could argue that they do not see it because it does not actually exist, but I think it is more a question of *visibility* and *seeing*.

The issue of visibility turns out to be a very complex topic, and to make the discussion manageable I will deal first, in this chapter, with some of the more simple and practical aspects. In the next two chapters I will explore some more complex but relevant concepts arising from twentieth century philosophy, which both address the issue of visibility and are worth the struggle needed to understand them, because they directly inform the bringing together of meaning and disease.

There are many reasons why we do not 'see' things, and avoidance of discomfort is one of the most important. Humans have a huge capacity for denial. Why face something that will destabilize us? Recently I was traveling in Mexico, and at times, when passing beggars supplicating for money, I found myself not wanting to see, and turning away, trying in a rather primitive way to make the 'phenomenon' disappear. Meaning-*full* diseases are most discomforting

phenomena because, even when looked at superficially, they destabilize the modern Western mind. Contemplated with openness, they
have the capacity to precipitate a crisis in our understanding of good
healthcare, and it is worth examining the reasons for this more closely.

Firstly, they challenge traditional classifications of disease. To a
large extent diseases have been divided into two categories. They
have been either 'physical' or 'psychosomatic.' This is such a tidy
idea—some illnesses (the psychosomatic ones) have a definite relationship with patient subjectivity, but the physical illnesses do not.
Meaning-*full* diseases disturb that tidy idea. We see **very** physical
diseases that are not regarded as classical psychosomatic disorders
and yet present as somatic metaphors. The popularly held crude distinction between *real physical* diseases with no 'psychosomatic' element, and those often reversible illnesses that are 'psychosomatic,' is
grossly inadequate to the task of categorizing physical illness with
meaning. This distinction is a direct result of the mistaken belief in
mind and body as separate compartments.

Secondly, somatic metaphors compel people to reflect on what a
'person' (with or without disease) actually *is*, to reflect on our fundamental nature. How can a meaning, a subjective idea, have a highly
specific metaphorically physical outcome in the body that is conven-
tionally seen as a sort of machine? New paradigms are called for,
and, in the end, we are impelled to ask deep questions about the
nature of life itself. Such questions have, of course, been pondered
since time immemorial by great thinkers and scientists, and they
must be considered here because somatic metaphors require us to do
so. At this time, when, in the eyes of many scientists and doctors, it
is expected that mechanistic or materialistic science will explain
every disease phenomenon, we have, in the somatic metaphor, a
major challenge to such materialist assumptions. I see somatic
metaphors every day. If we see them, it is a duty to point out their
implications. But changing one's paradigm is both discomforting
and very hard work.

Thirdly, Western healthcare provision is structured around
groupings of clinicians whose training, economic security, research
programs, and influence in the world, are in turn structured around
and dependent upon the biomedical model of disease. It would be
fundamentally disempowering for many of these clinicians to
include a mind/body or meanings approach when they do not

have the attitudes and skills to participate in anyway except to feel clumsy and helpless. Goethe, many years ago, said this more bluntly:

***

' ... people continue in error because they are indebted to it for their existence. They would otherwise have to learn everything over again, and that would be very inconvenient ... the only point with these professors is to prove their own opinion' [in Lukacs 2002, p. 108].

***

Fourthly, there are the issues of the clinician's emotional defensiveness. If, beneath his patient's presentation with genital inflammation there is a painful history of sexual abuse, or beneath another patient's back pain there is a burning anger at his family, then what does that mean for the clinician's own back pain, or headaches, or chronic mouth ulcers, or his wife's vulvo-vaginitis, or his daughter's Crohn's disease. There will be a natural resistance to thinking about his patients' meanings if it exposes him to his own uncomfortable meanings. How should he think about his son's early death from a brain tumour, and his friend's deteriorating multiple sclerosis, and on it goes. It is all too hard. It is easier to see disease in the machine model. I agree that it may be easier for the clinician, but is it better for the patients?

But I think the biggest issue for clinicians is the second cited above, the issue of paradigms. Put very simply, the phenomenon of somatic metaphor suggests that 'meaning' may be just as fundamental to disease as are the changes in cells and their biochemistry. It might even imply that 'meaning' or 'experience' is some sort of building block in the universe, as philosophers David Chalmers (1995) and David Ray Griffin (1998) suggest (we will address their views later). The important point is that though we have many phenomena that prompt us to acknowledge the importance of the mind/body connections, the phenomenon of somatic metaphor is a crucially different example that challenges our current models and paradigms sufficiently to make us consider different ways of seeing the world. Maybe this is the reason it is poorly recognized and hardly ever discussed.

We must also canvas the issue of prevalence and general relevance of meaning-*full* disease. Are these stories, such as those of Eunice and Katrina, just rare events, curiosities, mysteries that have little relevance to most patients? That is how we tend to treat phenomena that do not fit our customary understandings and conventional functioning. But dominant scientific paradigms, for example Newtonian physics, have collapsed around rarely observed phenomena that cannot be explained on the basis of conventional understandings. Thus even one or two cases of somatic metaphor demand attention. But rarity is not actually the case here. Somatic metaphors are reasonably common, a fact that adds to the argument for more general relevance.

I will now give a series of somatic metaphors showing a range of illnesses that reach metaphorical intensity. We need to keep in mind that we recognize a somatic metaphor when the *type* of physical disease, or its type of *presentation*, or the *organ(s)* involved, or its *body site* or *location*, appears to be *saying* the same thing, or expressing the same *meaning* or *meanings*, as the patient's own personal and subjective "*story*" expressed in the patient's *verbal language*, or in the *pattern* of the patient's important and meaningful *life events*. So, in the cases that follow, I suggest the reader try and 'listen' to both the 'story' data, or language, and the physical symptoms of the patients.

***

There are several ways of picking up 'meaning' of disease in a consultation. But, for me, listening to a person's *speech* is top of the pile. Let's go back to an example already mentioned: *the woman aged thirty four who complained of eight years of nasal congestion, facial soreness, and puffy eyes all beginning when her mother was diagnosed with scleroderma, a very serious disease that causes both skin and internal organ damage. I could not find an allergic cause for her symptoms. Discussing her mother, the woman says: "I will always grieve."* Note the congruence between her physical symptoms and her words. Grieving shows physically as tears, congested nose, and puffy eyes.

***

Listening to the person's speech may be enough, but evidence will accumulate in other ways. We can listen to not only the speech but also to the *facts* of a person's situation. For example, *a woman aged fifty complains of two years of chronic eye inflammation. She has been diagnosed with Sjogren's syndrome, an inflammatory disease that mainly affects mucous membranes typically causing symptoms of irritable dry eyes, and dryness of the mouth and the vagina. Actually, despite the medical diagnosis, she did not have any clinical evidence of dry mouth or genitals. She complains of exhaustion related to wandering around the world following her diplomat husband. She appears to want to come back home and settle down in her own house. She says: "I am tired, I can hardly open my eyes," and appears angry and frustrated. Her husband attended the consultation with her but would not allow further discussions.* Here I suggest that the woman's speech, the facts of her domestic circumstances, and her symptoms all tell the same story of tiredness, anger, irritability.

***

Sometimes the 'facts' seem to stand on their own. *A male medical technician, aged thirty seven, developed a heart rhythm disturbance, called a supraventricular tachycardia, while working in a stressful cardiology catheter laboratory. He then worked in operating theatre alongside a urology specialist who treats him rather badly and he developed an inflammatory bladder condition called interstitial cystitis. He attended my clinic for nasal congestion and catarrh for which we can find no allergic cause. We talk about the possible connections between his various negative feelings towards his previous employers and his various symptoms over the years, and the nasal symptoms subside.*

***

Sometimes it seems that listening to a *person's life history*, or to the *events that surround the beginning* of the illness, is enough to discern what is going on. *A woman aged fifty two complains of twenty years of bladder infections, bloody urine, vaginal discomfort, and excessive watering of the eyes. At age eight she endured sexual abuse. Her bladder problems had been continuous since her honeymoon twenty years before. In her speech she says: "I was such a go-er but I crash after sex; every now and again I give in to sex"; "I feel sickened."* The sexual abuse, the onset at the honeymoon, the bladder and genital symptoms, and the language, all suggest unresolved issues centering around the abuse.

***

'*Relationship*' is an important focus for listening and seeing. Most of the stories told so far imply that the patients' stories involve relationship issues. Let's now try listening specifically to some relationship issues. *For example, a woman aged twenty six complains of nearly three years of chronic diarrhoea and many medical investigations. It is clear that her husband works too hard, and that the symptoms began when they moved cities, and, more importantly, moved away from her father to whom she was very attached. She confessed that "I hate arguing" which might suggest that her strong feelings relating to the important men in her life were not being confronted adequately because of fear of conflict. I suggested these connections and a month later she returned for a follow-up consultation. Her symptoms had completely resolved after she told her husband "I am not going to be treated like shit any more." I had not suggested any such interpretation nor had I used language like that with her at the first consultation.*

***

The relationship issues that can underlie physical illness can be fascinatingly diverse. Most of us would have little difficulty in relating to many of them, because they represent the whole range of the vicissitudes of life we all experience as human beings. Consider another example. *A woman aged fifty four complains of six years of itchy welts on the skin, and an inflammatory bowel condition called Crohn's Disease both flaring each year in September. It turns out that she has a rigid workaholic husband, a lawyer, who has refused regular intimate relations with her. She lives in constant hope that their relationship will improve. At Christmas time when the family are around and she sees more meaning to her existence her hopes rise, that this year 'things will improve, and he will see sense.' But by September "my hopes begin to sag," and "how else can I show what I feel." She feels frustrated, angry, lonely, and afraid. Her symptoms break out again.*

***

Another relational example is *a man aged fifty two who has suffered fifteen years of severe tendonitis, a condition involving visible swelling and redness around joints. Curiously enough, this inflammation only occurred in tendons around joints that had been actively exercised a few hours before onset of the symptoms. There was a clear 'story.' By background and nature he was an extremely active man, a person whose identity was pretty well captured by action in the wilderness. But then he got married, which greatly limited his independence. He felt trapped, and limited to domestic duties. Significantly, it was always after domestic physical activity rather than wilderness physical activity that the tendonitis would emerge.*

***

The next question is how often do somatic metaphors and other meaning-*full* diseases occur? The answer is that we really do not know, mainly because we do not know when we are missing them, for reasons that I have spelt out above. Chiozza and Hay would say they occur much more frequently than I do. I have made an attempt to ascertain frequency in terms of the way I look at meanings and disease. The apparently high frequency of physical illness and patient 'story' associations in my practice led me to install a 'Medicine and Story,' patient-centred, clinical outcomes database,[1] in which I systematically collected my disease-with-meaning observations. Because there is no established classification system for disease and meaning I created a simple one based on patterns that I had come to recognise over the previous ten years.

In this tentative classification, the three main categories were:

1. *Physical disorders with apparent metaphorical or symbolic meaning* i.e., somatic metaphors, several examples of which have already appeared in the book thus far.
2. *Physical disorder with apparent meaning which is neither metaphorical nor symbolic.* An example of this might be the female who got severe headache starting at the various times in her life when she had been traumatised in relationship with men. In this case I might not be able to see a metaphor in the headache, but there appears to be a significant meanings element—the headache always emerges in relation to her experience of men.
3. *Physical disorder with onset apparently associated with significant emotional material or life events.* An example might be an illness coming on at a time of cumulative stress. If we dug further we might find all sorts of meanings but at a simple level it can be understood as some sort of breakdown in functioning related to the level of stress that many people would succumb to.

Having achieved some way of sorting the different kinds of phenomena into broad categories, I then systematically assessed each newly referred patient, with a physical illness, in terms of whether I could discern a clear and apparently relevant *story* element. *If I could discern a meanings element* the patient was assigned to one of the three categories defined above. We started entering patients into the 'Medicine and Story' database in late 1997, and by February 2001 had accumulated 513 patients[2], 311(61%) of which were in the three categories combined, and 137(26%) in the first category, that of somatic metaphor. This is the important point: A quarter of them were somatic metaphors.

Furthermore, 96 of the 137 somatic metaphor patients had what most physicians would regard as *real physical* not just *psychosomatic* illnesses. By this I mean they had diseases that could be detected by laboratory or other technological tests, or could be felt by the hand or seen by the eye of the clinician. These real physical diseases included diverse categories such as urticaria (also known as hives), vulvovaginitis, dermatitis, interstitial cystitis, recurrent tendonitis, recurrent sinusitis, anaphylaxis, myelofibrosis, colitis, Crohn's disease, and skin infections. The remainder (41 of the 137) would be classically described as *functional* (including pain, muscle spasm syndromes, irritable bowel syndrome, subjective oral syndromes like 'burning mouth,' aphonia or loss of voice, unexplained multiple symptoms, tinnitus, and many others), that is, not easily identified by physical examination or laboratory investigation of some sort.

The major point is that the 137 patients categorized as somatic metaphor constitute a very significant sub-group within the database. The actual frequency of somatic metaphor could only be settled if agreement were reached around what level of congruence between 'story' and the manifestations of physical disease qualifies for a diagnosis of somatic metaphor. I make the point again: the prevalence of somatic metaphors in my practice is based on *my* level of 'seeing.'

Rigour demands confronting the possibility, that all this apparent congruence between meaning, language, circumstances, and physical illness could be mere chance and coincidence. I accept that possibility, but do not believe this is the right or even likely explanation, and I challenge the all too common tendency to jump to that conclusion. Many people, especially clinicians, do this as if by reflex. The interpretation, that what I am seeing is merely a mixture of chance and self-delusional projection is an easy and, I believe, understandable but ultimately self-serving way to deal with the phenomenon of meaning-*full* disease.

I suppose the final restraint for most of us brought up in a scientific ethos is that meaning-*full* diseases cannot be explained by any of the familiar models. They are therefore unlikely to be true phenomena. Such a stance puts the conventional paradigms of explanation in the unlikely position of having all truth captive. Foss (2002, p. 26) points out "it is the nature of scientific practice to make the premises of the ruling model self-validating." Typically a very creative scientist will make an observation of a new phenomenon, and this will eventually generate a good scientific theory to explain that phenomenon, and lay the basis for further work by many other scientists. Unfortunately such a theory all too often becomes a 'site' from which anything that does not fit the theory is excluded, not considered, or rendered invisible, even inconceivable—to do otherwise is to risk invalidating the theory. Thus, a new 'better' theory always eventually tends towards exclusivity. This is what Foss is referring to in his statement above. We will see later that it is true that the assumptions of the current scientific models cannot easily accommodate meaning-*full* disease, and are profoundly threatened by phenomena that demonstrate a link between illness and meaning.

If we examine the nature of this threat, we find it is not just a matter of having the tidy sewn-up measure of the world that science proffers. We disregard or deny all sorts of provocative and destabilizing material for many reasons, including those cited above. It is a natural thing to want to maintain the coherence of our belief systems and models, and to avoid threatening the institutional structures we have developed. We all tend to minimize any chance of loss of personal competency, and want to maintain recognition of our hard-won expertise. We are hardly likely to choose routes that threaten our career structures. We like to be right rather than wrong, and it sticks in the craw to discover that I might have been blind to a whole level of reality. In that event my supposed mastery turns out to have been an illusion, or at least very partial. Who wants to acknowledge that?

While I accept that rigour demands we entertain the sceptical position in respect of somatic metaphors, I also believe that rigour demands serious consideration of the implications of somatic metaphors. The phenomenon of somatic metaphor has greater impact when we discover how common it is, even though, if it were rare, it would still demand explanation.

NOTE

1. CORM-Qualcare. The Clinical Outcomes and Resource Monitoring software was developed by Professor I. Marks, at the Maudsley Institute, London, for monitoring behavioral therapy outcomes; see also Bullmore et al. (1992). The software was customised for our 'Medicine and Story' database use.

2. In 2000 I assessed 362 newly referred patients with physical symptoms of many kinds. I assigned 130 (36%) to the Medicine and Story Database, and the figures given in the main text suggest that 61% (79) will be in the 3 main disease and meaning categories combined, and 26% (34) will be somatic metaphors. Many of my referrals have typical allergy clinic conditions, such as hayfever, for which there are very effective physical treatments, and, at this point, I make no attempt to take a meanings approach with these. In my first book (Broom 1997) I spell out the pragmatics of when a meanings approach is most appropriate in the present medical climate.

CHAPTER EIGHT

Meaning-*full* disease and the *lebenswelt*

Many of us take for granted that the way we 'see' the world is *the* way to see the world, or that our peculiar kind of seeing is entirely adequate to the way the world really is. This stance has some advantages. It can enable us to achieve a sense of coherence in our world-view, and a degree of equilibrium with a sense of control over our lives. Therefore, if opening our eyes to other ways of seeing the world causes us difficulty, why on earth would we do it? But the reality of meaning-*full* disease suggests that opening our eyes may lead to unforeseen benefits well worth transient discomforts and disequilibrium.

I will address the category of the *visible* and the activities of *seeing* in more detail, and in different ways, in the next two chapters, but they must be introduced here, too, because of their relevance to our subject, the *lebenswelt*.

The twentieth century phenomenologists, beginning with Edmund Husserl (1859–1938), had a lot to say about how we apprehend reality. Husserl spoke of a *natural attitude*, which is the state in which we 'simply accept the world as a background or horizon for all our more particular experiences and beliefs' (Sokolowski 1999). In other words it is natural for us to take our seeing for granted, and to squeeze the phenomena of the world through the sieve of prior beliefs, which are thus imposed upon, and shape, the phenomena.

I suggest that the 'natural attitude' as it pertains to science involves an extreme focus upon the thing-ness of things, with a consequent loss of other realities, certainly a loss of focus upon meanings. In much of science this way of seeing, this natural attitude, involves a presupposition of the world as fundamentally material, and leads to a constriction of seeing. As a consequence, meanings and story in meaning-*full* diseases are inevitably invisible.

Husserl argued that for us to see the world the way it really is we need the *phenomenological attitude*, which leads us to stand back from natural automatic beliefs and attitudes, the *natural attitude*, and adopt a 'reflective consideration of intentions and their objects'(ibid p. 405). The phenomenological attitude involved an endeavor to minimize restrictive assumptions, and to try and see things as they are. As a consequence of the way they started to observe the world, and in reaction to the natural attitude of science (the thing-ness of things), the phenomenologists argued that to really understand the world we have to focus less on 'things' and more on 'the meaning and being' of beings. It should be clear why this appeals to me as an observer of meaning-*full* diseases. It calls upon the clinician to step back from the usual way of seeing patients and their disease presentations, to metaphorically blink to clear the clinical eye and vision, and to look again at the data floating to the surface in the clinician/patient encounter. Let me give an example of just such an encounter occurring during this period of writing.

***

Charlotte, a 28-year-old school teacher, was referred for a relatively rare but well-recognised skin condition called cold urticaria, which is characterized by itchy welts on any skin exposed to cold temperatures. Cold urticaria is usually satisfactorily managed (as per the medical *natural attitude*) by cold avoidance, by education regarding the risk of swimming and other cold exposure situations, and with antihistamine drugs.

I was also asked to address a breathing problem as a separate issue. She was experiencing episodes of difficulty in breathing, which she recognized as being associated with anxiety. The breathing problem involved a feeling "that I am not getting out of the air that which I need." It did not appear to be asthma or

any other type of common respiratory condition, though phenomena such as 'air hunger' and tightness of the chest are common concomitants of anxiety. The content of her anxiety always
involved the possibility of something dreadful happening to her
parents or brothers. The breathing problem would arise as she
brooded on being separated from them, or losing one of them.

The story opened up wide when she said she had had these
curious breathing problems as a child from about age six, and
she emphasized that they only occurred during the *winter*
months. She would often call her parents to her bedroom complaining she was not getting enough air. Physicians were consulted but nothing physical was found. Her mother believed that
the problem began after surgery Charlotte had had when aged
six. She was admitted with suspected appendicitis but a 'growth'
on the ovary was found and removed. They were informed that
the growth was a *vestige of a twin that had died in utero.*

I noted that Charlotte was born full-term in April, indicating
conception in July the previous year. July is mid-winter in New
Zealand. I then started to wonder aloud with Charlotte about
this apparent conjunction between the cold urticaria, the winter-
time breathing problem starting at age six, the removal of the
twin vestige at age six, the current persistent anxieties about separation, her July conception, and the possibility that her twin
didn't survive beyond the winter after conception. She was
somewhat startled, but responded saying her life was dogged by
July-ness. She met her husband in July, got engaged in July, then
married in July, and was planning an overseas trip in July. She
nearly died in a car accident in July (age 17), and her father had
surgery for cancer in July (when she was age 18). Her favorite
number was seven.

***

Putting aside questions of how this conjunction of data might be
explained until a later chapter, let's consider it in the light of our
two attitudes. Taking the orthodox medical 'natural attitude,' most
of the data in the story would not have surfaced in a consultation in
respect of either the cold urticaria or the anxiety-related breathing
symptoms. The usual medical style of questioning would not
engender such emergence, and the assumptions of the clinician
would lead him/her to suppress the data if they did perchance
emerge. If, on the other hand, one takes the 'phenomenological

attitude,' and suspends judgment, and moves away from diagnostic labels and disease conditions, and explores the phenomena *as they surface in the interview* in the spirit of the 'meaning and being' of beings, one starts to see a strange (sic) mixture of data in which a totally unexpected pattern emerges, a pattern of deep feeling about loss, separation, winter, and cold. Her life has an over-determined quality around these issues, as if they pervade her whole being, or life.

Of course it is never possible to approach anything without presuppositions, and I would have never proceeded to ask her about these aspects of her life unless I had assumed that meanings and matter were deeply interpenetrative. But, relatively speaking, I did step back from the medical natural attitude and started to look for the relevance of very diverse phenomena as they floated to the surface in the real world of our encounter.

This takes us to our subject, the *lebenswelt*, or life-world, which was one of Husserl's most important concepts. If we want to see the world more the way it is we need a radical change of attitude, where we turn from 'the realm of the objectified meaning as found in the sciences to the realm of meaning as immediately experienced in the *lebenswelt* or "life-world"' (Kockelmans 1999). Moving from the natural (scientific) attitude to more of a phenomenological attitude we see this life-world.

This notion of the life-world is very relevant to the 'seeing' of meaning-*full* disease. The life-world is the real, experienced, lived-in world. It is a much richer world than that of mere objects, or that defined by the objective existence of things. The life-world *gives rise* to the scientific world, but it is much more than the world described by science. There is no disconnection between the scientific world and the life-world; it is just that the scientific world is an aspect of the life-world. As Solokowski (ibid p. 407) puts it, this

***

world has its own structures of appearance, identification, evidence, and truth, and the scientific world is established on its basis. One of the tasks of phenomenology is to show how the idealized entities of science draw their sense from the life-world. Husserl claims e.g., that geometrical forms have their roots in the activity of measuring and in the idealization of the volumes, surfaces, edges, and intersections we experience in the life world.

***

Quite simply, the life-world is a rich, multidimensional, experienced reality of which the scientific world is a part-representation, a reduction, or an abstraction. The life-world is of such a nature that it does have geometrical (and other) forms, such as volumes, surfaces, edges, and intersections, which therefore have measurable aspects. But the life-world is not *fully* comprehended in all its richness by science, because science is the methodology by which the *physical* forms of the life-world can be explored. The subjective meanings in the life-world are not visible to science. Science is a methodology of examination of the stable, structural aspects of the life-world by measurement and experimentation, and, thus, a scientific narrative of the physical aspects of the life-world is possible. At the risk of pressing the point too strongly, science should be seen as the development of a systematic approach to a *certain aspect* of the life-world, made possible because, in a crucial aspect, the life-world *is semi-stable*, has *form*, and is therefore *measurable*. But science is not a complete approach to all aspects of the life-world.

Let us now turn from science to medicine. Unfortunately medicine has come to be based almost entirely upon what *science* can 'see,' resulting in a 'dead-matter' view of the person. Reiterating the point again, as a methodology of examination of the stable structural elements of the world, science does not, cannot, and should not be asked to 'see' all aspects of the life-world. As a corollary, Western medicine, which is dominated by science, does not see meaning-*full* disease. If we see the task of science to examine the structural aspects of the world then it is legitimate for it to ignore other aspects of the life-world. If we see medicine as also only committed to examining the structural aspects of humans then it is legitimate for medicine to ignore meanings. But actually the task of medicine is to bring healing, and healing encompasses far more than the structural aspects of humans. Therefore it is not legitimate for medicine to fail to see meanings, which happens because of its ideologically-driven, over-commitment to the scientific natural attitude.

We need to develop this notion of the constriction of medical 'seeing' a little further and, as always, a story helps. I remember my first week of medical training. As a callow nineteen year old, wearing a short white coat, and carrying a scalpel and tweezers, I, with one hundred and nineteen other medical students filed nervously into the huge anatomy dissection room at the University of Otago Medical School, in Dunedin, New Zealand, with its unadorned plaster walls, the clinging odor of formalin, and twenty white-draped cadavers laid out on stainless steel plinths. We spent hundreds of hours over the next two years, in teams of three, dissecting the pallid, stiff cadavers. We systematically deconstructed the physical body, but the consciousness, vitality, stories, meanings, reactivities, and individuality of the person were absent. I do not remember at any point discussing the former 'life' of our cadaver with my student colleagues. We learned a 'dead matter' perspective of that person, and of persons in general. The rest was invisible; we did not seek it out, nor were we encouraged to do so. The point is that from the earliest stage in training, the body, as a physical mechanism (and diseases as manifestations of mechanistic breakdown), is highly visible to the modern clinician, but the meaning-*full* context in which the body functioned, and in which diseases emerge is invisible.

In training as doctors, we learned to 'see' persons and disease in certain restrictive ways. In the anatomy dissection room we explored the 'volumes, surfaces, edges, and intersections,' the structured, anatomical forms of the body in all their physical intricacy and measurability. It is a perspective that has considerable utility in the medical vocation, but it is a perspective that renders meaning invisible. Medical resistance to the conjunction of meaning and disease, which is so much greater than that of the average lay-person, may *in part* be due to this powerful early conditioning of medical students: that, ultimately, the body is a dead matter-based machine to be taken apart, and under certain circumstances to be reconstructed.

The argument thus far pre-supposes that there *are* other aspects of the life-world outside the rubric of conventional scientific description, and, by extension, there are other aspects of persons outside, but relevant to, the conventional medical descriptions of disease. This is where meaning-*full* disease helps, because there are so many remarkable clinical examples that make the concept of the life-world very compelling. We can recall the case of Margaret, from chapter one, who was raped at age thirteen and many years later developed bleeding from the genital, urinary tract, and breasts in relation to the stirring up emotional material originating in the rape episode. It seemed that the physical and non-physical experiences were all entwined in a way that could never be adequately described by the natural attitude of science.

In my first book (see Broom 1997, pp. 2–3) I detailed the story of a woman (patient T.) who, in her early thirties, developed a precancerous condition called leukoplakia, which manifests as a whitish abnormal appearance of the lining of the mouth. Over the following twenty years she required seven surgical interventions, including reconstructions of the tongue because of cancer. I will summarize some of the key elements here because they are very relevant to our current discussion.

In the course of my first consultation with her, I discovered that her father, who was a dentist, had died by suicide in his early thirties, and that my patient's mother had inexplicably accused the daughter of causing her father's death. T. developed the precancerous mouth condition when she was precisely the same age her father was when he suicided. We uncovered a persistent shame at having 'caused' her father's death. During a remarkable but brief series of therapy sessions, she addressed this issue of shame, and the precancerous condition, which had dogged her for many years, disappeared.

It seems impossible to do justice to this story by resorting merely to science with its limited boundaries. The story captures the dialectics of the visible and the invisible, of the natural attitude and the phenomenological attitude, and of the scientific world of physical forms and the life-world which is a messy, rich, mysterious amalgam of objectivity and subjectivity. We *can* look at the story from both scientific and life-world vantage points. As a scientifically-trained medical clinician, using the terminology of semi-stable, structural forms which I have already introduced above, I can look inside the *volume* of her mouth. The white plaque on the *surface* of the oral mucosa has a typical appearance or form that we call leukoplakia. As an oral surgeon I could watch it conscientiously over many years, and would do so, because I know that eventually it will lead to mouth cancer. When it does transform into cancer I act promptly and efficiently, with all the skills accrued through the history of development of oropharyngeal surgery and my own personal training. In all this I have a very sophisticated scientific 'gaze.' I remove the parts of her tongue and pharynx that have become cancerous. As a result of this, the *structure* of her mouth is radically changed, and she has to learn to speak again. But the fundamental problem of leukoplakia persists, and she develops a further cancer requiring more surgery. In all, she experiences twenty two years of good Western medical observation and treatment of the 'scientific body,' but does not get treatment of the 'life-body.'

In a different narrative, and by marked contrast, I get to see T. at the end of that saga, and I consider the patient as a 'life-body.' I explore her 'life-world.' T. initiates the consultation around the fact of the medically-observed leukoplakia and the secondary cancer—thus we begin the session with the problem of the physical mouth, as perceived in the scientific world. But our divergence from this constrained view begins very early in the session. Listening to her carefully I hear language suggesting something else is going on. She has come because she wants to 'get rid of **it**' (ibid p. 2). I suspect that she wants to get rid of the leukoplakia *and* also something else that is somewhat less visible. Of course, we might mutter at this point 'let's just keep it simple, it is just so obvious that all she wants is to get rid of the leukoplakia and the cancer!' But such muttering emanates from the scientific world of forms, and the natural attitude that that world engenders. In that perspective the forms are the beginning and the end of the matter.

The life-world is different. It includes the forms *and* other matters as well. Therefore, I asked myself, what is this **it**? Of course, it is the leukoplakia and the cancer, but in the life-world it is always going to be more than that. The life-world and the life-body are always more than their scientised structures and forms. And so our exploration of her life-world and life-body begins. We have no idea what we are about to find, but I assume that her early life, her parents, her feelings, her experiences, and her body are all part of her life-world, relevant to one another, and therefore relevant to her disease. In our exploration we uncover many things: unhappy parents; mother's accusations; a father who commits suicide; leukoplakia of the mouth; the condition begins at age 33; father died at 33; and father was a dentist.

In the 'scientific world' perspective this list of diverse elements is just an assortment of unrelated data. They are different categories of information that have no real place together. The fact that they present a persuasive congruence must be ignored, or glibly explained away as coincidence.

But in the life-world view it is legitimate for these data to assemble in the one place because that is where they originate. They have a natural coherence. In a life-world view of the patient we have a life-body, not just a scientific body. Body and experience are a unity. In contrast to the dissection room perspective, in the life-world and life-body much more of the patient's life and experience becomes visible, and it is to this concept of 'visibility' we now turn.

CHAPTER NINE

Meaning-*full* disease and the 'visible'

M uch is said in this book about that which is seen, and that which is not seen. It was Maurice Merleau-Ponty (1908–61), the eminent French psychologist and philosopher, and another major figure in the development of twentieth-century phenomenology, who really emphasized the notion of 'visibility,' in his manuscript *The Visible and the Invisible* (1968), which was published after his death. He has much to say about the body, but readers accustomed to thinking in terms of a body separated from the mind, or the body as an object separated from its capacity for subjectivity, may find some of Merleau-Ponty's language rather strange. He focused on the lived body, or the body subject, or the bodily nature of the human subject. This emphasis on the conjunction of body and the human capacity for subjectivity is captured in the idea that the body is a *chiasm*, a crossing-over place that combines subjective experience and objective existence.

In an attempt to find a categorisation that captures these two aspects he employed the word *flesh*. It seems that he was trying to transcend the limitations of our Western notions of the body. He says, for example, that when we touch one hand with the other, the 'flesh' (in the way he uses the word), is both a form of *subjective experience* (the experience of touch) and an *object that can be touched*. These two aspects are actually indivisible, but we know them or reflect on them, even construct them, as separate categories. I both *feel* my hand, and *have* a hand that feels. My hands, and by extension my body, have, therefore, an ambiguous status as *both* subject and object. Let's analyse this distinction from the vantage point of visibility. At one moment my hand is 'visible' as *subject*, and then, at another moment, my hand is 'visible' as a thing or *object*. It is the peculiar nature of our bodily existence that it allows this double aspect. We are subject and object at the same time.

Our bodily existence is more than a 'dead matter'-based, object-like existence. I *have* a hand and I *feel* my hand. We see the *chiasm*, the crossing-over place, in the experience of hand and the fact of hand. Subjective experience and objective existence mingle together. Diseases, too, represent crossing-over places, of objective and subjective aspects of the patient's reality. They are a chiasm or crossing-over place of both meaning and biological dysfunction. Whether we actually *see* both the objective and subjective aspects of disease depends on what we as clinicians and patients make visible and invisible. The willingness of the observer to see is crucial. Our fundamental experience as existing beings *is* as both subject and object. We work our experiences over using the processes of conscious reflection, dividing the experience up into separate categories, and we find ourselves in one moment visible to ourselves as subjects, and in the next moment visible to ourselves as objects.

Some of this may seem rather theoretical, but it is very relevant to meaning-*full* disease. Merleau-Ponty's concepts of *flesh* and *chiasm* fit well with the idea that diseases carry *both* objective and subjective aspects, that diseases are meaning-*full*. Whether we see both the objective and subjective aspects depends on what we make visible and invisible, and it is clear that the subjective aspects have been rendered invisible by our dominant ways of looking.

Returning to the story of the patient with leukoplakia referred to in the previous chapter, we can see how, in one focal plane, we constitute her story as one of anatomy, of a mouth with volume and surfaces, of visible pre-cancerous and cancerous conditions with characteristic objective physical features, and of a physical nature that can be managed using surgical techniques, that, in turn, are an extension of the physical form of her suffering. But, if we move to another focal plane, what comes into view is the patient's subjective story of father-as-dentist, of death by suicide, of feelings of responsibility for his death, and of poignant symbolism in relation to the timing of the onset of her illness. In the first focal plane the physical elements are visible and the subjective elements are invisible, and in Western medicine we habitually handle disease in this way.

At this point the issue of visibility could be construed as mostly to do with what we *choose* to look at, of what we *allow* to be visible. We have already seen that that can be a relatively simple matter of refusal, for paradigmatic reasons, to allow the subjective elements into the field of view, or because we do not want to be disempowered in our roles as experts in the field of medicine. But, for the phenomenologists, the notion of visibility is much more than an inability or refusal to see. It is also a matter of the complex relationship between the seer and the seen.

When it comes to what we actually see, or the *visible*, there is an extraordinary and mysterious relationship between that which is visible and the person who sees the visible. It turns out that the 'object' of vision and the seer are both intimately involved in constructing this phenomenon of seeing, rather like the sea and the land reciprocally create all the phenomena of the seashore. Merleau-Ponty makes the point (see Baldwin 2004, p. 249), in commenting on the relationship between so-called 'things' and the 'seer' of things, that there is not a hard and fast 'thing,' or object, out there, observed by an 'empty' seer. The seer can never see the 'thing' in its nakedness, because the 'gaze' of the seer 'clothes' the thing with its own 'flesh.' What is this 'flesh' of the 'gaze' of the seer? We know his concept of 'flesh' includes the objective and subjective aspects of being. Clearly the influence of the 'flesh' here is a combination of, firstly, the way the eye works in a physical sense, and, secondly, of subjective influences upon seeing. The subjective and objective nature of the seer, who is thus 'flesh,' hugely influences the seer's perception and experience of the thing out beyond the seer.

Merleau-Ponty uses the seeing of a certain tone of redness as an example. Let's say that, with our gaze, we fix upon *one* red color in an array of other reds and other colors. This 'fixing' upon one particular redness involves the participation of many other variables:

***

a naked color, and in general a visible, is not a chunk of absolutely hard, indivisible being, offered all naked to a vision which could be only total or null, but is rather a sort of straits between exterior horizons and interior horizons ever gaping open. ... If we turn now to the seer ... The look ... envelops, palpates, espouses the visible things. As though it were in a relation of pre-established harmony with them, as though it knew them before knowing them ... so that finally one cannot say if it is the look or if it is the things that command [in Baldwin 2004, p. 250].

***

Again, this is difficult without considerable reflection, but it is the last sentence that captures the point most powerfully. The relationship between the seer and the seen, or visible, is always a co-creation. Nothing is entirely constructed by the seer, and nothing is seen entirely in its naked reality.

We may be able to clarify this further by turning to another sensory modality like that of touch, within which we discover a plurality of realities, even though they are really of one reality. In the sense of touch we have three components: firstly, the touching that can, for example, differentiate the sleek and the rough; secondly, the touching of a thing as something in a space; and, thirdly, a

***

touching of the touched, when my right hand touches my left hand while it is palpating things, where the "touching subject" passes over to the rank of the touched, descends into the things, such that the touch is formed in the midst of the world and as it were in the things [in Baldwin 2004, p. 251].

***

In this, he is obviously intertwining our experience of ourselves as subject and object, and showing how, at one moment, a hand is 'visible' as subject, and then, at another moment, 'visible' as a thing or object. And it is the peculiar nature of the body, or the *flesh*, or our bodily existence, which allows this.

How do we ground these ideas in relation to meaning-*full* disease? Turning again to the patient with leukoplakia, we can say she is 'flesh,' and her condition of leukoplakia is 'flesh.' Thus, I can make the physical aspects of her leukoplakia visible in one moment, and then make her shame at having 'caused' her father's death visible in the next moment. And it is not just the patient who is 'flesh.' So am I, as the clinical observer. Subjectivity and meaning resides in her disease, and in me also. I bring a meaning-making capacity to her disease. I, too, am 'flesh,' a subject body, and as a subject body I act on the world to constitute reality. As Merleau-Ponty puts it, this subject body is 'the sole means I have to go unto the heart of things, by making myself a world and by making them flesh' (in Baldwin 2004, p. 253). But, as an observer of the patient's story, of her meaning-*full* disease, I am not the *sole* constructor of the meaning. If I were, it would be a story of shame causing disease solely *originating in my reality*, and *imposed* on her. I actualize the emergence of the meaning *because* I see her as subject and object, as 'flesh,' or indeed as she really is.

This issue of who is responsible for the emergence of meaning is a difficult one to tease apart. Let's return to the story of Charlotte, which I introduced in the previous chapter to contrast the 'natural' attitude with the 'phenomenological' attitude. As we opened our eyes to whatever data was floating to the surface of the clinical encounter we found ourselves seeing a patterning involving cold, winter, separation, and loss; issues that pervaded various dimensions of her life-world. But a sceptic will claim that I went looking for such data, and that I was able to 'create,' from her data, patterns that suit my assumptions about the world. In other words I imposed my constructions on Charlotte. To address that accusation one could say many things. But, according to Merleau-Ponty, there is actually no escape for any of us whatever our paradigms; all clinicians participate with their patients in the construction of a view of the disease reality. If my patients get better by collaborating around a meanings construction, in what sense is that fundamentally more doubtful than healing resulting from the construction a surgeon co-creates with his patient to remove a bowel tumor? Secondly, why would sceptics prefer to see me as a meanings determinist, that is, as a clinician determined to force a meanings pattern on disease, and to search the patient's data to discover such a pattern? Maybe the alternative view of me, that I am a holist who allows meaning into the clinical scenario, and as someone who is open to seeing meanings patterns, is intolerable, because ultimately it implies that the sceptic's paradigm of disease is inadequate. Certainly, Charlotte's pattern would never have emerged unless I was willing to entertain meaning as a factor in illness. To go further than that and claim that I forced it into the clinical encounter is to deny my experience of that encounter. Firstly, I had no preconceived notions as to any connections between her cold urticaria and her anxiety. I have seen many cold urticarias and never seen any such association. Secondly, she spontaneously took me back to the beginnings of her breathing problems at around age six and offered the data of her mother's view that her surgery had something to do with it. And so it went on. My experience was more of her leading me into the patterns of her phenomenology rather than me leading her data into my deterministic world of meaning-making.

But there is no doubt that, as 'seer,' I participated in the emergence of this pattern. We all play a large role in constructing clinical realities, and in chapter five I expressed concerns about imposing patterns of meaning on diseases. But biomedical clinicians are at risk in the opposite way, of closing down on meanings data, and thereby blindly imposing a non-holistic framework upon their patients.

Seeing everything is impossible. Seeing enough is desirable. We have choices. We can choose to see the object or the subject or both, though maybe not both at exactly the same time. The important thing for the theme of this book is that we do not have to render the subject invisible; and it follows that we do not need to render meanings of disease invisible.

Merleau-Ponty is emphatic that the subjectivity and the objectivity of the flesh are indivisible:

***

the body ... is neither thing seen only nor seer only ... there are two circles, or two vortexes, or two spheres, concentric when I live naively, and as soon as I question myself, the one slightly decentred with respect to the other. ... [in Baldwin 2004, p. 255]

***

This is a very interesting point, because he is saying that, as soon as I focus on myself as an object I decenter my attention and become directed towards myself as an object, and lose focus upon myself as subject. In other words I lose my sense of reality as a subject. We not only do that to ourselves, *but also to our patients*. Returning to the patient with leukoplakia again, we have a medical history of some twenty years of 'de-centered' attention, of her disease as a vivid, very significant and serious 'object.' And yet in the space of a few minutes it was possible to re-focus and discover her as a person and her disease as 'subject,' equally vivid and very significant.

It is important to emphasize that Merleau-Ponty's notion of the 'flesh' is nothing like the common use of the term:

***

'The flesh is not matter, is not mind, is not substance. To designate it, we should need the old term "element," in the sense it was used to speak of water, air, earth, and fire, that is, in the sense of a general thing, midway between the spatio-temporal individual and the idea, a sort of incarnate principle that brings a style of being wherever there is a fragment of being. The flesh is in this sense an "element" of Being. Not a fact or a sum of facts, and yet adherent to location and to the now. Much more: The inauguration of the where and the when, the possibility and exigency for the fact; in a word: Facticity, what makes the fact to be a fact. And ... what makes the facts have meaning.' [in Baldwin 2004, p. 256]

***

Thus we have, in the "flesh" a much richer, wider view of the embodied person, properly capturing our capacity to sense and be sensed, to be both subject and object, to participate in the construction of our unique reality. And, note that the flesh 'makes the facts have meaning.' Meaning, or the capacity for creating meaning, appears to be a fundamental aspect of the flesh, which of course we would expect, given the fact that the 'flesh' has an inherent subjectivity.

There are many other aspects to the issue of visibility, one of which is, quite simply, that, as ordinary observers, it is impossible to focus on everything without being overloaded or overwhelmed. That which we render visible, is merely 'the surface of an inexhaustible depth' (in Baldwin 2004, p. 260). We are always choosing what we see, and there are circumstances when certain styles of habitual choosing allow us to function efficiently without being overwhelmed. But the systemic failure of medicine to entertain the 'subject,' to recognize the 'flesh' in respect of physical disease, represents a scandalous blindness to reality inimical to the care of patients. In many circumstances this blindness, and often a conscious refusal to entertain a role for human subjectivity in disease, reaches a level of professional neglect and culpability. As I write I have just reviewed a patient where the invisibility of his subjectivity has contributed to longstanding, and, I believe, unnecessary suffering:

***

John is forty-three years old and has suffered from severe 'migraine' from age eleven. It occurs about two monthly, and is unresponsive to all medications. He is rendered non-functional for three days, two of which he usually spends in bed. As an infant he had very severe eczema, and he has been assumed to be an 'allergic person.' He returned to New Zealand after twenty years of being settled in the United States where he had an excellent social network. The reasons for returning were his 'closeness' to his mother, and her deteriorating health. He developed quite severe asthma the day after he arrived back, and had had it most days in the six years since then. It gets much worse with exercise, and he has noticed it is triggered by 'stress.' Even more distressing was the development of violent diarrhoea, again beginning within days of returning to New Zealand. It is much worse if he runs, and has therefore been labeled 'runner's diarrhoea.' His headaches, asthma, and diarrhoea were much worse after his mother died in somewhat distressing circumstances. His hostile relationship with his father then became much more obvious. He has strong fears that his health might deteriorate like his mother's did, and that he might meet the same fate. He has not established a good social network in New Zealand. While he has strong feelings about many things he has no one to talk with about them; his partner 'just doesn't understand.' He presents in the clinic as having strong feelings, but keeping tight control of them. He has been sent to me to sort out his allergies. The history was not particularly suggestive of allergy, and skin testing showed no evidence of allergy.

I framed his illness as follows. He was brought up in a caring healthy environment, enjoying a very close relationship with his mother. He establishes an excellent social context in a foreign country and enjoys good health except that every now and again he 'explodes' in the form of headaches, which I saw as being, in his case, an outlet for pent-up feelings or needs in a person who has learned to contain them within himself. After twenty years overseas his primal links with his mother motivate a return to New Zealand. Several aspects would predict this might have been risky for him: He was rather too identified with his mother, and was returning to an old, overly close, pattern of relationship; he has a fundamentally hostile relationship with his father who was envious of John's relationship with his mother. By leaving the United States John was leaving behind crucial well-established support network. Within hours of arriving in New Zealand he lost control of his airway and his gut. He recognizes (though his clinicians do not) that when his feelings get stirred up (or he gets stressed) so does his asthma and his diarrhoea. His symptoms are understandably much worse as his mother gets very ill and dies. Running seems to make the asthma and diarrhoea worse, but is not the main or sole cause of the symptoms. It seems that vigorous physical exercise activates the nervous system in such a way as to make his lung and gut instability worse.

***

In this formulation I have made *some* of the mindbody aspects visible. We do not have fine detail, but there are plenty of pointers in the story to encourage the idea that if the emotional and relational aspects could be better managed his body would be less explosive or out of control. What should be done? My experience leads me to be quite hopeful. Firstly, he needs to have his feelings acknowledged, heard, and talked out properly. He is a person who will easily bury them as 'trivial,' or, with encouragement, come forward with them and put them into verbal language, thus making it less necessary for him to 'explode' in the body in the form of asthma, diarrhoea, and migraine. Secondly, he needs to register more clearly to himself when he has such feelings, and when they are building up, and thus have a chance of dealing with them differently. He needs to find people with whom he can share his feelings, and it may be necessary to discover new and more successful ways of doing that with his wife. The two of them are in a rut, and acknowledging that together may lead to new opportunities. He has a powerful need for a more active social network, and there may be things he could do to reconcile with his father.

In my experience, working with him in this way is highly likely to lead to much less in the way of physical symptoms. The point of course is that he has had seven years of medical diagnoses and physical treatments for his asthma, diarrhoea, and migraine. It has been assumed that he is just an allergic-type person. The medical treatments have been only marginally helpful. The subjective 'story' has been totally invisible, despite the fact that it creates so many therapeutic options.

This notion of visibility has many ramifications and as we reach for ways of imagining the presence *together* of subject and object, of disease and meaning, there are other resources we can call on, including, for example, Japanese concepts of the body, which I will review next.

CHAPTER TEN

Shifting awareness and different kinds of body

When it comes to illness most Western patients do assume a separation of mind and body, a stance that frequently blocks opportunities for healing. In many instances this is simply a culturally-derived lack of awareness of the possibilities of a holistic perspective. But, in some, it is much more than that. In the first case described below the patient *insists* on a physical approach to his symptoms. In his responses we can discern a desperate search for a cure, but also very limited *physicalist* assumptions of disease causation, and a *determination* to confine the illness within physical parameters. There is a rigidity in his stance that cannot be easily penetrated. We have already discussed in chapter two the rather similar rigidities seen amongst biomedical clinicians. These rigidities have quite varied origins but, in the patient below, the rigidity seems to be rooted in the patient's underlying terrors of psychological vulnerability. Fortunately many patients are much more flexible in their thinking than either this patient or many clinicians. With relatively little encouragement they allow an expansion of their awareness.

***

Jonathan, aged 35, with a four-year history of groin pain, sore throats, muscle spasm headaches, and fatigue, consulted me, asking very specifically for an 'allergy' approach to his symptoms. He had enjoyed good health for most of his life, and, until he became ill, there had been no necessity for any examination of his understandings of health and disease. Over the four years of the illness he had received many orthodox (specialist and non-specialist) and non-orthodox investigations and treatments, including antidepressants, acupuncture, removal of all his mercury dental fillings, and a variety of herbal remedies. He was a handsome, urbane, articulate, apparently confident person who crowded the consultation interaction with internet-based information, diagnostic labels, and working assumptions about his illness acquired in many previous consultations with other health professionals, most of which were predicated on the belief that his illness was *purely* physical. Nevertheless, he described himself as a 'driven' person, and it was easy to discern that he was a highly performing individual, very disdainful of weakness of any sort, and afraid of psychological concepts. The illness originally began at a time when he was struggling with a decision to return to New Zealand from Australia, and in the immediate context of two work redundancies, and very unstable social relations. Gentle enquiry around these aspects led to a sharp retort that 'my symptoms are *so* physical that they *cannot* be related' to such life events. Later in the session he hinted at some awareness of his mindbody connections, but these concessions were hurriedly overlaid with statements like 'there is nothing wrong with my head.'

***

Simply stated, it was my opinion that this man was unlikely to get the healing he desired unless he could risk awareness and acknowledgment of the 'story' aspect of his symptoms. He had been heavily reinforced in his preferred physicalist framework of illness by all of the physically-oriented responses he had sought from clinicians. His defensive need to avoid any perception of weakness or vulnerability meshed in with these purely physical constructions of his symptoms. The assumption was, and had to be, that this illness was purely physical. This rested on a prior assumption that mind *is* separate from body, and for that reason it was valid to consider an illness as purely physical.

Reflection upon this common tendency to construct mind and body as thoroughly separate gives rise to several issues. How much does the perceived separateness simply reflect our human need to have a manageable way of dealing with different aspects or categories of our experience? We might say that we function, manage our lives, on the basis of a *thought and language-derived dualism*. Thus, the separateness of mind and body may be seen as a practical outcome of active *human* consciousness in the world. Even if we grant that possibility, as we must, in the light of post-modern theoretical contributions to our understanding, how much is the normal (sic) perceived level of separateness of mind and body *exaggerated* by Cartesian and other influences in Western culture? And maybe we are so stuck in this exaggeration that it is difficult to imagine any other construction? In other words, have we created extra problems by over-doing an underlying pragmatic working dualism?

Returning to the patient mentioned above, my initial endeavors involved excluding an allergic cause for his symptoms, and, then, expanding his awareness of himself, and the factors underpinning his illness. Such an expansion of awareness is crucial for patients and clinicians if we are to grasp the new therapeutic possibilities arising from understanding the meanings of illness. But it is not just a matter of patients allowing themselves get past their defenses to enter an expanded awareness. We also need an expanded awareness of the fact that there are other possible constructions of the healthy and diseased lived body way beyond those provided by the narrow Western biomedical model. Where do we turn?

In the Asian religious, cultural, and philosophical traditions there are some very interesting and radically different views of the ways a person exists *as both subject and object*. This is potentially relevant, because meaning-*full* disease very much draws our attention to ourselves or our patients as both subjects (experiencing persons) *and* objects (biological organisms with measurable organ dysfunction).

I turn then to a brief review of the writings of Shigenori Nagatomo. In his book *Attunement Through the Body* (1992), Shigenori draws on the work of Ichikawa Hiroshi and Yuasa Yasuo, who are contemporary Japanese philosophers in roughly the same general phenomenological tradition as Husserl and Merleau-Ponty.

As we have seen in chapter eight, the phenomenological method includes a turning away from *things* to their *meanings*, from a preoccupation with the science of objects, to a focus on 'the realm of meaning as immediately experienced in the "life-world"' (Kockelmans 1999, pp. 664–6). This shift, or *epoche,* is very relevant to meaning-*full* disease where there is both a conjunction of disease as physical 'object,' and disease as 'meaning' and a need to shift one's attention from one to the other.

When I work with patients with disease, I employ a phenomenological method continuously. Typically, I start with my attention on the 'thing' of illness, the disease manifestation, and then I slide my attention seamlessly towards the 'meaning' of the same illness, whilst still holding them together in the same clinical time/space. Throughout the consultation I am moving seamlessly backwards and forwards, backwards and forwards, attending to the physical, 'object,' disease aspect in one moment, and then attending to the subjective 'meaning' aspect in another moment; in a zigzag way I am gradually building a picture of multifactorial, multidimensional emergence and perpetuation of disease in this person in front of me.

The key to successful mindbody practice is this ability to shift one's gaze flexibly from the body dimension to the mind dimension and back again, and again, and again, as necessary. When working with some patients this can be a very difficult matter indeed, as in the case of Jonathan above, or that of Peter presented in chapter one, to which I turn again because the process of my encounter with Peter illustrates both the rigidity of narrow physicalist awareness, and the possible movements in awareness that may occur when a clinician is determined to confront the rigidities *for the sake of the patient.* The fine details of Peter's story are very important and, thus, I repeat it here in its entirety:

***

During the first consultation, while we talked, he lay on the floor being unable to sit on an ordinary chair. The other most obvious features were the exquisite tenderness of his back muscles on examination, his profound suspicion of me, and his huge anger towards his third party funding source.

His 'story' can be told another way. He was (in his view) the unwelcome last-born of numerous children, and the only one who had failed academically. He established his self-esteem through sporting prowess. As a child his angry temperament was notorious, to the extent that he was given a special nickname (not disclosed here) to reflect this. He left school early, with a strong sense of academic failure, which he compensated for by *excellence in sport*. The 'broken back' caused by the mountaineering accident symbolized the destruction of his capacity for sporting excellence, of his worth and competency. In his view, surgery on his back might just *complete* the crippling process. Thus surgery was a terrifying prospect. Because of his pain he was unable to re-establish himself in any sort of sporting activity. As a person who was an academic failure he could not imagine developing alternative non-physical 'head' skills to replace his loss of physical competence. He was enraged with his funding organization because of the pressures they put on him, and afraid they would terminate his support, and leave him stranded. They and the various medical specialists concerned with his care were almost entirely focused on his physical body, and had no understanding whatsoever of what was going on in his subjectivity. Not only was the latter divided off, it was also invisible.

After acting as a mediator with his third-party funding source I did nine sessions with Peter. My notes give some idea of the process: 'we have both found the intensity of the encounters almost intolerable.' He raged on endlessly about his funding institution. It was extremely difficult to get him to focus on his anger issues, and how his anger might be perpetuating his back pain. At the ninth session, in utter frustration, I informed him I could not work with him unless he agreed to stop talking about his problems with the funding source, and focused more upon the role of his anger in his back pain. I thought I had lost him but he returned three weeks later, willing to stop focusing upon the funding source. A remarkable process of change ensued. Seven sessions later he was running his own business, which involved considerable physical activity. He was continuing to get some minor pain if he did too much lifting, but he was essentially living a normal life.

***

Here we have a man with back pain triggered by traumatic injury, in which the physical (injury) factors and the subjective factors (the anger) are so profoundly mingled that we actually feel drawn away from any separation of disease and meaning, towards a deeper uni-fied layer where the physical and the subjective exist together as one rich amalgam of aspects. In the story we can see how the object-body (as the patient's injured physically tender back), and the subject-body (as the angry man in danger of losing his value), seem to dis-appear as separate entities, and become *one*. But Peter does not see it that way, at least for a start. He has a very restricted awareness of the dimensions of his problem. Here is *his* version of what hap-pened, provided in a letter sent to me after his recovery (reprinted with permission):

***

"*To whom it may assist.*

After 10 years of 4am pain wakings I found myself sitting in front of a psychotherapist Brian Broom. Prolonged sleep deprivation had, and was taking its toll on me and I was very angery about that, as well as frustrated and many other feelings twisted into a knot which was find-ing a home on my injured lower back.

On meeting Brian (as he insisted I had to call him) he told me that I seemed "frustrated and angry." this mainly made me frustrated and angryer. Not a good place to be, angry and getting angrier.

I found my first 6 sessions with Brian very hard work. No answers to my problem were coming forth from Brian and this fuelled my predickament more, pushing me further into the corner I found myself in. Like a injured animal trapped by its injury.

I told Brian the knickname my 2 brothers and 2 sisters had for me when I was young, "..............." (deleted to help preserve anonymity, but the nickname referred to his angry tendencies). *This Brian told me was the root of my problem. I figured this man is expensive to see and he must know his stuff, so I regretted for awhile telling him the knickname and then thought "It's the truth" and then had a good look at my anger and why it was in me. As most things my anger was due to a number of factors.*

My injury was one part of the problem. Some childhood stuff that I had ignored for years as is often the case. So instead of saying stuff this I had a close look at myself from the other side of the fence meaning from the outside looking in.

I figured that the reason Brian wasn't giving me any easy answers because there aren't any and I had most of them hidden in my anger somewhere.

So on I looked, very hard work but I didn't like my other options. Loosing Brian's help and going back into the corner of the padock was harder than looking at myself. Mainly my feelings towards things like my pain, my restrictions, my future, plus many more I don't wish to put down here.

As I spent more and more time looking at all these feelings (a hard thing for a Kiwi 60's born male to do) but the more I studied my feelings the less pain I found myself in.

Once I started waking in less pain I was less angry about waking in pain which made me rest better and the back injury had some time to heal and on it went, less stress, less pain, more improvement, DAA, DEE, DAA, DE DA

I must finish here, at the moment, got to do homework for my Local ....Operators License, and my new future.

With great thanks,

Peter"

***

The difficulties encountered by Peter and myself are all too obvious. There was a massive problem of lack of awareness of the factors perpetuating his symptoms. There were intense negative feelings creating an almost impenetrable barrier to progress. We teetered on the brink of failure, and, eventually, I resorted to risky confrontation; the relationship survived this confrontation and the outcome was wonderful.

To establish the awareness needed in meaning-*full* disease we battle with many factors. Difficult dynamics between the clinician and the patient can prevent safe progress to the awareness needed. Some diseases are so complex in their origins that teasing apart the contributions of the physical and the subjective dimensions presents a huge challenge which may defeat even the most experienced mindbody physician. And there is the major problem of the culturally accepted dissociation of the mind and body dimensions. On top of this there is the tendency to give priority to one dimension or the other, a manoeuvre itself based on assumptions of mind and body separateness. In the individual clinical case the management of all these factors can be very difficult.

Nevertheless, despite all the difficulties encountered, it becomes obvious that Peter's problem emerges from a unified whole, or a 'deeper layer,' from which we can abstract categories like 'injury' and 'anger.' Responding to him as such a 'whole' delivers the result he has been waiting ten years for. And it is to this 'whole' that we must direct some more attention.

In the phenomenological method of Shigenori, Ichikawa, and Yuasa, we see the *lived body* in multidimensional ways, and in ways that are so different from those based on our assumptions of person-as-biological-machine-*plus*-mind that we (as Western thinkers) can become almost disoriented. But the *central* idea in Ichikawa's work is not particularly disorienting. It is that in our deepest 'layer' we are unified, and it is out of this unified deeper layer that our experience of ourselves as having a subject-body and an object-body emerges.

***

My "object-body" and my "subject-body" are inseparably united in their deeper layer, and cannot be separated clearly and decisively, except through intellectual abstraction. [Ichikawa 1979, in Shigenori 1992, p. 26]

***

This means that separateness is secondary or derived, it is an intellectual abstraction, and it is something *we do* to the data. We thus need to be careful that we *see* the more primary unity. Every day, in meaning-*full* disease, I see this amazing inter-wovenness of physical and subjective elements, to the point that I cannot but conclude they are truly aspects of each other within a unified whole. We can say then that the physical and subjective elements in meaning-*full* disease are 'inseparably united in their deeper layer.'

Such a view does not deny the existence of differentiation. Ken Wilber in his illuminating book, *The Marriage of Sense and Soul* (1998) provides a very helpful commentary on the related issues of differentiation, dissociation, and separateness. He argues that our capacity to *differentiate* categories of mind and body (and other dimensions) is an achievement of evolved consciousness, or, as he puts it, a *dignity* of modernity. On the other hand modernity's *dissociation* of them has been a *disaster*. By dissociation he means the radical separation of mind and body to an extent that *we can no longer see* that they really are just different aspects of one another.

The first patient described in this chapter, Jonathan, showed not only a marked tendency to dissociate mind and body, but also a secondary tendency to negate any role for mind. Dissociation is followed by negation. Whilst, of necessity, he lives life as a unified whole, he also dissociates, negates, suppresses, and distorts important dimensions of that whole and as a result he has symptoms he longs to resolve. It is all so ironic. Negation leads to the illness, which leads to a search for healing, but only within a Western biomedical healing tradition that insists on the negation.

William James was concerned about this issue of the *whole*, or the *deeper layer*, and argued, in his *Essays in Radical Empiricism* (1912) that there is not really a separate mind or a separate body, and that we have to go beyond these categories to something *neutral* in between. This is the

***

view known as 'neutral monism' that denies the differences and the duality and asserts that there is only one kind of 'stuff,' and that is neither the mind nor matter but something 'neutral' in between [Monk 1996].

***

Many people have stretched for a way of describing the 'deeper layer.' From an entirely different tradition, Ray Grigg (1997), in his *The Tao of Being. Lao Tzu's Tao Te Ching Adapted for a New Age*, says 'the uni-verse is reached only by putting back together the multiverse' the implication being that the real nature of things is oneness, despite our tendency to abstract this oneness into parts and categories, into mind and body, particularly when we talk about them with one another.

Let us now examine, through the perspectives of Ichikawa, Yasuo, and Shigenori, this concept of body and mind, of subject-body and object body, of disease and meaning, as *abstractions* rooted in *'their deeper layer'* (Ichikawa 1979 in Shigenori 1992, p. 26).

It would be a fair summary of Ichikawa's view to say that we are *bodied beings*, though he does not use that actual terminology. In the term *bodied* I am avoiding the currently popular term 'embodiment,' which in its literal meaning implies that the body is a vehicle for something else, something more abstract, for instance the mind, and I do not like that emphasis. The 'embodiment' literature reflects a largely helpful impulse to ground the mind as embodied rather than as some separate epiphenomenon of the body and brain. To that extent it combats mindbody separateness. But it still has the 'feel' of Western dualism, which I am trying to avoid. More than that, it feels to me that in many of the 'embodiment' constructions the mind is being returned *to the body*, to the physical, *which is therefore implicitly the ultimate reality*. In other words, the embodiment endeavors are ultimately physicalist and materialist, as we might expect given the general development of Western culture from the Enlightenment onwards. This concerns me because I am not ultimately a materialist, and I do think it is possible to pursue the 'whole' without ending up in a fundamental materialism, or for that matter, a fundamental idealism.

But I am not one to negate the physical. I do believe that, as living entities, we are *deeply* physical, that all our reality has a bodily aspect to it. That is different to saying that we are *ultimately* only and primarily physical. Therefore I prefer the term *bodied* rather than *embodied* when I refer to the fact that the unified person is physical through and through.

From Ichikawa's phenomenological vantage point we experience our body in two ways. There is

***

the subject-body, that is the body we live immediately and directly from within, and the object-body, that is the body we objectify through our external sense perception. [Shigenori 1992, p. xvii]

***

The body is not a material object upon which the human spirit acts. That is the Western dualistic view. The concepts of body and spirit are actually abstractions for crucial aspects of our lived bodied experience. The "fundamental structure" (ibid p. 5) of the bodied being includes the dimension of spirit, such that the concept of spirit can be pulled out as an abstraction. In a real sense the body is body and the body is spirit. I, as spirit, do not have a body, like some ghostly owner of a biological machine. I am bodied through and through. I am spirit through and through. I am subject through and through.

Underneath the experiences of subject-body and object-body is a lived body scheme that synthesizes and unifies the two, a

***

lived unity or oneness between the subject and object, between the interior and the exterior [ibid p. xviii].

***

Whatever way we choose to characterize it, whether as the 'deeper layer,' or as the 'fundamental structure,' or as the 'neutral' stuff in between, we see the experience of subject-body and object-body emerging from it.

The *object-body* is our common experience of the body as a 'thing.' We can use an example from Ichikawa (see Shigenori 1992, p. 20). I can touch my foot with my hand, and experience that foot momentarily as a thing or object in relation to my touching of it. In this way then it is an *object* or thing, which I, as the subject-body, touch. But notice that the foot also participates in another way as part of my subject-body, because there is another experience which can be easily identified. I, in my foot, experience myself as a *subject* being touched. So my foot is *in experience* both object and subject, and depending upon what I focus on I can separate these two experiences. *I am both object-body and subject-body.*

But there are certain circumstances in which they cannot be separated. Shigenori (1992, p. 23) points out that when the palms of the hands are pressed together in the traditional prayer position it is impossible to divide the two experiences of subject-body and object-body; they seem to fuse, they become one, seemingly suggesting that the separation into object-body and subject-body is a function of how we manage the various aspects of experience that emerge from the 'whole.'

But there are real differences. The *subject-body* is something we live or experience 'from within, grasping it immediately' (ibid p. 6). The hand experiences itself as 'subject' touching the foot, the 'object.' We can isolate the foot as an object (that is, as part of the object-body) but the foot still experiences the touching as 'subject.' The subject-body embraces both the physical and the mental dimensions. As a phenomenon it does not feel like an aspect or activity of a separate mind. It is a truly bodied experience.

The subject-body is related to the experience of consciousness. Consciousness as an experience is a highly complex category. There are things we are very conscious of, and things that we are barely conscious of. In the same way we are not evenly aware of all aspects of the subject-body, and much of the time we hardly attend to some of its aspects. Thus Ichikawa says that in our *bodily experience* of consciousness there is a continuum from a 'bright horizon' of consciousness to an 'obscure, hazy horizon' of consciousness (see Shigenori 1992, p. 8). Some things are in the front and some in the back of our consciousness. Many features of consciousness (or *cogito*), such as active thinking, vivid conscious memories, many cognitive or thought functions, and immediate physical tasks upon which we are focusing, are clearly represented at the *bright* end of the continuum. But Ichikawa argues that cogito extends right through the whole bodily continuum to the obscure, *hazy* horizon of consciousness.

There are some aspects at this 'hazy' end that we can only see, so to speak, out of the corners of our internal 'eyes.' They may become more obvious with trained attention (as for instance in various meditative states), and there may be many unconscious cogito elements only accessible to a gifted few, or in dreams, or manifest indirectly in behaviors, and, of course I would say, in *diseases*. And it is that latter point that is most relevant here. Meaning-*full* diseases are often a representation in the *immediacy of the body* of 'stuff' that is otherwise active at the hazy end of consciousness. The disease makes us aware of something out of order. If we look hard at it with open minds the nature of the dis-order may become quickly obvious, or it may not.

Readers will be aware that I have drifted from the terminology of consciousness to Ichikawa's *cogito,* which includes, in this usage, the categories we know of as conscious, preconscious, and unconscious. For Ichikawa, at every point cogito rests in the body; it is bodied, there is no disembodied cogito. There may be more or less awareness of certain dimensions or aspects at various points in this continuum, but body and cogito are truly present throughout. For me, the term cogito carries various categorical possibilities such as information, meanings, knowing, as well as consciousness, which by its very nature refers mostly to the 'information' aspect at the 'bright end' of the continuum.

The subject-body is different from the object-body. While it is definitely bodily, it does not have a definite shape in terms of the way the object-body can be seen, touched, and measured. The potential for measurement is a chief characteristic of the object-body, and it is the arena of scientific and medical endeavor. But the subject-body is different. It is definitely experienced, and lived immediately from within, and while it cannot be measured it has a 'kind of "extension and volume as its fundamental tone"' (see Shigenori 1992, p. 9) What does that mean?

As I sit here I am very aware of my hands on the keyboard, the position of my object-body leaning towards the monitor, the sun shining on the screen, and the movement of the dog out of the corner of my eye. My eyes and my sense of touch create an object world that we easily recognize. This is my object-body. But as I move to another level of perception I am aware of myself within, as both a physical and subjective being, occupying a definite space and volume, tightening, shrinking down, limiting myself somewhat, focused over the keyboard, and then moving to a different mode, loosening up, expanding, letting go, wandering off, freeing myself, becoming something else, taking a deep breath, stretching my limbs, unwinding, looking up and out rather than in and down, freshening myself, shaking off the burdens of thought and typing. This is the subject-body. Some might call it the phenomenal body. It is full of physicality and subjectivity, action and awareness, and it extends into and occupies the world. I think that is what he means by positing 'extension and volume as its fundamental tone.'

Ichikawa's perspective is therefore based on *these phenomena that we actually experience.* We experience ourselves as an object-body and as a subject-body, and these emerge from or are embedded in a unity or oneness. Much of this oneness can be characterized as a 'preconscious' lived body scheme, which is prior to the everyday consciousness that divides experience into subject and object, and, in the context of this discussion, into subject-body and object-body (Shigenori 1992, p. xviii).

The central idea governing this discussion is this: *At the level of the phenomenology of ordinary bodily experience, as discussed by these Japanese philosophers, who do not have meaning-full disease in mind, we discern exactly the same pattern of closeness of subjectivity and physicality that we see in meaning-full disease.*

Let's ground all this by referring back to Peter's back-pain. We can talk about the back pain using Ichikawa's concepts? Firstly, we can consider Peter's object-body, which is similar to the body under consideration by the orthopedic surgeon who wishes to operate on Peter. From the object-body perspective, Peter did get injured in a certain sporting incident, he does have a measurable abnormality of his vertebral column, and he does have some tenderness over his lower back. But, within that narrow conceptualization, Peter remains a conundrum to both the surgeon and the insurer as to why he has been so severely crippled for so long. *The object-body construction is not sufficient to explain all that happens to Peter.* There is a mystery that dissolves if we accept the notion of subject-body, and particularly if we understand that subjectivity, or cogito, extends right through the continuum of the bodied being. One cannot have Peter as a living bodied being without taking account of his subjectivity. By definition then, the anger and fear are in some way present in Peter's back—they have to be. In Peter's case the cogito involves the fear and anger attendant on the sense of profound threat to his identity. The back injury and the threat are 'one.' They should not be seen apart. Body and cogito are co-continuous. In such a model there is a clinical expectation and assumption that both the fear and anger, and the consequences of physical injury, will be manifest in his back. And that is exactly how it presents to us, phenomenologically, in the clinic. This allows me, as the clinician to exercise that zigzagging mode of observation I described above. I am free one moment to focus up on the structural abnormalities in his lower back, and then in the next moment to consider his back as an expression of anger. I am constantly shifting my awareness. The co-continuous nature of body and cogito allows and, indeed, demands that. Moreover, the use of a clinical approach predicated upon such assumptions results in a relatively rapid healing outcome. Admittedly there was a huge struggle initially, but it is fairly obvious that the struggle in part arose from the damaging assumptions of a clinical approach limited to the view of the patient as merely an object-body.

Ichikawa limits himself to an analysis of what we actually experience in our everyday consciousness of our lived bodies. Certainly, and in line with the phenomenological attitude, he does ask us to relinquish our natural attitude and attend to some things we usually ignore or take for granted, such as the difference between the subject and the object-bodies. Nevertheless the aspects we have been discussing are fairly readily accessible to everyday consciousness. From these phenomenological observations Ichikawa proposes a unified field from which emerge our experiences of ourselves as both object-bodies and subject-bodies in seamless conjunction. To speak of seamless conjunction and also to speak of both subject and object bodies seems paradoxical, but in reality the paradox dissolves when we realize that *the separateness has more to do with how we focus upon or attend to things.*

In like manner the kind of data and categories we see in meaning-*full* disease emerge from the same unified field. We listen carefully to people talking about their illnesses, and just as we can discern the subject-body and the object-body, so we can discern the patterns of physical disturbance in seamless conjunction with the patterns of associated and relevant meanings. And just as it is possible to focus upon the object-body and ignore the phenomena of the subject-body, so it is possible to focus on the physical manifestations of disease and fail to attend to relevant subjective meanings. In orthodox medicine this is normal practice. The 'natural attitude' of medicine in relation to Peter with his back pain was quite simply a matter of injury, medications, possible surgery, physical rehabilitation, re-training for new types of work, and simplistic blaming of the patient for not complying with this grossly inadequate conceptualization of what it was to be this particular patient with a back injury. Bringing the subject and the subject-body into clinical focus is vastly more efficient in his rehabilitation.

We have seen that Ichikawa views the subject-body and the object-body as abstractions, as one of the ways we organize our conscious experience of our more fundamental 'deeper layer.' But, as Wilber emphasizes, the organism does differentiate, and modernity's understanding of, and emphasis upon, differentiation has been one of the 'dignities,' one of the great achievements of human civilization. Therefore, continuing to track Shigenori, I want to consider 'body schemata.'

CHAPTER ELEVEN

The scheming body

Many patients present to doctors with symptoms that cannot be categorized within conventional diagnostic classifications, and, very frequently, patients feel rejected and devalued because the clinician, out of a constrained perspective and sense of powerlessness, reacts by pushing the patient away. The problem is that many symptoms do not 'map' clearly onto the usual ways clinicians have of seeing the body. The patient's disorder cannot be explained according to the doctor's ordinary understanding of anatomy or disease processes. Here is a typical example:

***

John is aged thirty-nine, and was a valued administrator in a financial services business where growth had been phenomenal, and staffing had not kept up with the work-load increases. He took on more and more responsibility and became progressively exhausted. His wife said of him that 'he can never say "no!"' Apparently this was a long-standing pattern, seen in all aspects of his life. Eventually an unexplained episode of deafness in one ear took him to his doctor, who was unable to provide a satisfactory explanation. He returned to work, and suddenly collapsed. He described the sensation as an 'incredible heaviness'; and 'it was like my spine was collapsing, shrinking down until it was only two inches long.' He was conscious during this first event, but unable to move his limbs, which he described as 'paralysed and heavy.' When he recovered from the paralysis the deafness had gone. He had intensive neurological investigations but no definitive diagnosis was made, and three years later, at the time of consultation with me, was chronically fatigued, unable to work, and was having three to four collapse episodes a day, all rather similar to the original collapse. He hesitated to leave the house and frequently got collapse episodes when left alone. He was confined to home doing gardening, which he enjoyed greatly. He was very angry that the medical profession was dismissive of his symptoms, because he did not fit into their usual diagnostic classification systems and because they were powerless to help him.

***

We will see later, that utilizing different ways of 'seeing' the body, we do have creative options, but orthodox medical models are very restricted in their abilities to help people like John. The *first* problem is that many *symptoms* presented by patients like John do not 'map' easily onto clinicians' diagnostic categories. The *second* problem is that most of such patients have meaning-*full* diseases, and the *meanings* aspect neither 'maps' onto Western models of disease, nor onto most of the diagnostic categories employed by clinicians. Because, within these constraints, there is no easy way of explaining how specific meanings come to be represented in the structure of the body as illness and disease, many people 'intuitively' reject the role of meanings in disease. It is clear that we need some different ways of seeing the body, so that we can understand better its relation to meaning, and to achieve this there are two important obstacles that must be overcome, or at least considered.

The first obstacle is being addressed from different vantage points in every chapter of this book. It is the problem of how to see persons as non-dualistic wholes, when *we have learned to see them as combinations of separate things*. With respect to this, I am saying, quite simply, that the problem is partly of our own creation, because we have come to believe that mind and body are separate when they are not. I have already acknowledged the widespread and growing effort in academic circles to conceptualize persons as unified non-dualistic entities, and to reverse the severe dissociation of mind and body that has occurred during the last few hundred years. But, following Wilber (1998), we must acknowledge the helpful consequences of differentiation of dimensions of human functioning, and distinguish these benefits from the prevalent damaging consequences of severe dissociation and partition, which is seen particularly in medicine, and which is our focus.

The second obstacle is the way we think about how different aspects of the body are organized, and how *we* divide the body up into 'schemata,' or, using Wilber's terminology, how we have learned to *differentiate* aspects of functioning of the body. When we try and relate meaning to our customary ways of organizing our thinking about the body, we find that Western medicine, which pivots its activities around the object-body, provides us with extremely limited options. The question becomes whether there are other options.

My view is that the two obstacles are, in part, created by our form of consciousness. I actually wonder whether a *thorough-going* non-dualistic conceptualization is actually beyond the reach of ordinary human consciousness, simply because of the nature of thought and language. The activity of 'talking about' something is, in essence, a dualistic activity in the sense that talking always involves selecting one aspect, and therefore not another aspect. It is true that much language-making involves the putting of things together. Metaphors, symbols, and other kinds of imaging involve the drawing together of elements. But thought and language in another essential aspect involve the dividing of life into *categories*. Indeed language rests upon the dividing of things. We are not capable of handling data by thought or language without dividing things into categories. But that is a different matter to saying everything is fundamentally divided or dualistic *in its original state*, before we thought or talked about it. Therefore, part of our problem is the dualistic, category-making nature of language and, by extension, all theorizing. As Loy (1988) says:

***

"… it is the *experience* of non-duality which philosophizing obstructs. From such a perspective, the problem with philosophy is that its attempt to grasp non-duality conceptually is inherently dualistic and thus self-defeating." (italics mine)

***

In our context, the second obstacle becomes, essentially, the question of how meaning may map onto the organization of the body in its recognizable patterned circuits, systems, or schemata. In the previous chapter we saw that in medical practice we focus upon systems of body organization in relation to the *object-body*. This is primarily a focus on the flow of information in relation to *structure*, or anatomical systems. This does not turn out to be very helpful with respect to meaning-*full* disease. Quite simply, using an example from the last chapter, how does Peter's anger in response to *threats to his identity* map onto his damaged spine? In an orthopedic surgeon's world it is a matter of *disorganized anatomy*, a view which is essentially a limited object-body perspective.

As we will see, we do have well-described organizational systems within the object-body framework, and the question arises as to what sorts of organizational systems emerge in relation to the *subject-body*, and whether these might be more relevant to meaning-*full* disease.

To indicate some possibilities I will draw on Shigenori's (1992) treatment of Yuasa's (1986) *body schema*, which in one respect are similar to the biomedical model. Biomedicine maps disease onto the anatomy and structures of the object-body. Yuasa's information systems and information flows do mostly map onto known body structures and physiological pathways. The great difference is that the structures and physiological pathways represented in Yuasa's body schema are essentially organized around *experience*, the experience of the subject-body, rather than *structure*. That is, the information he maps onto body structures is the information of experience. And that is indeed a radical way of looking at the body at least from a Western medical perspective, but it derives logically from the fact that we do experience ourselves not only as object-bodies but also as subject-bodies. Let's take it step by step.

The medical profession has organized itself into specialties according to the body viewed as *structure*. Let's consider the cardiologist who, in his anatomy-based scheme, focuses upon the heart as a sophisticated mechanical pump. Of course he is preoccupied with its function, but that is always an extension of the heart as a physical structure. His concern extends from the macro-structure of valve to the micro-structure of the electrical circuits coursing through the heart muscle, and the hormone receptors on individual cell walls. While he maintains a fairly restricted focus upon the heart, as a system that can be isolated from the rest of the person, he is certainly interested in certain aspects of kidney function and lipid metabolism, because of the ways in which the functioning of these structures and systems may impinge on the structure and function of the heart. His focus is undoubtedly a focus on structure, which we might say is rooted in our experience of ourselves as object-bodies. His treatments consist of modifications of structure, and consequent function, either by macro-techniques such as surgery, or micro-techniques via the influence of drugs. In this schematisation of the body, the body as object-body is the perception of body that underpins the clinician's reality; experience, and the subject-body is relatively invisible.

The subject-body is hardly in view, but there is the odd bright spot. Cardiologists are conceding that 'funny things' do happen. For instance, a February 2005 issue of the prestigious New England Journal of Medicine ran an article on the "Broken Heart Syndrome," citing 19 cases of patients with serious heart dysfunction following sudden emotional stress (Wittstein et al. 2005). Remember the story (in chapter two) of the man who had his heart attack in the emotional aftermath of a sports final, and the presenting cardiologist alluded to the stress factor in passing. Very recently a 52 year old woman was referred to me with a formal diagnosis of the 'broken heart syndrome.' The story was that her husband had recently informed her he was homosexual, and that he would be leaving the marriage. This was a huge shock. A few days later she had a cardiac arrest, and was resuscitated by her husband. She was rushed to hospital and over the next thirty six hours had a series of cardiac arrests, and eventually required a temporary cardiac pace-maker. Full investigations showed no permanent damage, and she was diagnosed by a cardiologist as having the 'broken heart syndrome.' But these concessions, in the face of persuasive circumstantial evidence, are exceptional. In the object-body scheme of things cardiologists, generally speaking, highlight the body-as-structure-and-object, and render the body-as-subject-and-experience invisible, despite the fact that cardiology clinics are full of patients that could do with a meanings approach.

We do not need to pick on the cardiologists; the same commentary applies to all specialties. Consider my own, which is clinical immunology. In contrast to the heart, which is such an obvious large structure, confined to one anatomical site, the immune system is an army-like defense system largely based on cells and molecules dispersed throughout the body. But it does have a definite macrostructure. Many of the immune cells take origin in the bone marrow, some get processed as they pass through a small neck gland called the thymus, and others develop and multiply in the many lymph glands around the body. These lymph glands are connected by a 'plumbing system' of lymphatics, which are rather less obvious than blood vessels, and the immune system uses both the lymphatics and blood vessels for transport of cells and fighting molecules such as antibodies. The fundamental capacity of the immune system is to recognize 'foreign-ness,' and then combat the threat posed by the foreign invasion.

The point here is not a tutorial on the immune system, but to emphasize how easy it is to isolate the immune *system* as a body scheme, and to see it as truly isolated. As an immunologist I am trained to think 'horizontally'; that is, I think about the connections *within* the system rather than about the connections *with* other body systems that have been equally isolated. It is actually a little harder to do that with the immune system because, being the sort of system it is, its 'war zone' is always an organ 'belonging' to another specialist, for instance the skin of the dermatologist, the lung of the respiratory physician, the kidney of the nephrologist, the nose of the ear, nose, and throat surgeon, and the gut of the gastroenterologist. Nevertheless, the immunologist's eye is set towards immune function as it relates to immune system structure, even though most of the structures in his system or schema are tiny elements such as cells and molecules. Certainly there is a substantial and growing body of research in the field of psychoneuroimmunology, exploring the phenomena of psychological influence on the immune system, but this hardly penetrates to the level of everyday clinical immunology practice. And even more certainly, most immunologists have little concept of the immune system as functioning within the *subject*-body.

We can see then that Western medicine has organized itself into a style of clinical practice that has certain clear features: The body is organized or divided into systems according to physical structure or anatomy; the function and dysfunctions of these systems is best seen in structural terms, whether it be a matter of injury or genes; treatments consist of modifications of structure either by macro-techniques such as surgery, or micro-techniques via the influence of drugs; and there is minimal room for *experience* alongside *structure*, in other words the object-body rules, and the subject-body is invisible.

The stage is set now to consider Yuasa's *body schema*, which, in contrast, refer to information systems and information flow, largely focused around the phenomena of *experience*. It is important to reiterate that these experience-based schema or systems are mostly not seen as separated from body structures and physiological pathways. Yuasa is therefore trying to retain *structure* within his field of view, while focusing upon schemata based on *experience*. Western clinicians focusing on structure do not generally give *experience* the same respect. The great illusion of the Western medical specialties is the assumed validity of exclusion of experience, subjectivity, mind, or consciousness, from one's consideration of the causes of disease construed as a structural dysfunction. The reverse illusion would be that we can reasonably exclude structure in our considerations of the organization of the body as seen via a focus on experience.

It will gradually become clear what Yuasa means by his body schema, but the term *schema*, itself, arose in the nineteenth century with Kant and Wernicke, and was promoted early in the twentieth century by the physiologist Henry Head, and more recently by theoreticians from linguistics, philosophy, and psychology. There is no universal agreement as to the real nature of schemata, but contemporary thinking emphasizes the importance of the role of the *body* in determining the way in which we structure *mental* schemata, as we saw in chapter three when discussing the work of the linguists (Lakoff and Johnson 1999). We could get bogged down in theorizing, but for my purposes it is sufficient to emphasize the notion of schemata as a way we have of conceptualizing the complex, organized, recognizable *patterns* of functioning, and handling of information, by the subject-body and the object-body. For example, the cardiovascular or immune systems could be considered schemata (in the object body) under this definition.

Moreover I will ground the discussion of schemata in actual cases of meaning-*full* disease, which are likely to be more powerfully illustrative of the notion of schemata, and how they operate, than a thousand words of abstraction. Readers who want a less specific application of Yuasa's body schemata can access Shigenori's or Yuasa's original texts. But the intent here is to show how body schemata cast light on meaning-*full* diseases, and how meaning-*full* disease may incidentally shape ideas about body schemata.

Yuasa proposes *four* information body *circuits*, a term which I see as roughly synonymous with organizational levels, or body schemes. Once again this is a categorizing, dividing approach, and we must remind ourselves that it is us, the observers, who are doing the dividing. Yuasa's circuits could be seen as analogous to the cardiovascular and immune systems, in that they are to some degree isolatable, though they are not, in reality, isolated from either the other circuits, or indeed the structure of the object-body. I will introduce them all briefly, and then further expand on them as they might relate to meaning-*full* disease.

The first is the external sensory-motor circuit which we recognize in many ordinary life situations, such as the experience of touching a hot object and withdrawing the hand. A stimulus is followed by a motor action. This is the easiest of the four circuits to summarize, though we will soon see its apparent simplicity is an illusion.

The second circuit is the circuit of coenesthesis. There are two divisions to this circuit. *Kinesthesis* refers to experience that has to do with *the state and position of parts of the body, and a readiness and preparedness of the body for action.* Kinesthesis underpins the functioning of the sensory-somatic circuit. We experience the sensory-somatic circuit in clear consciousness, but the physical experiences of the kinesthetic circuit are at the edges of our consciousness. Subjective aspects of the kinesthetic circuit are said to include thinking and willing. *Somesthesis* is another aspect of coenesthesis, to do with *the state of our internal organs.* In 'a normal healthy condition' this circuit 'recedes into the background, first behind the circuit of kinesthesis, and then behind the external sensory-motor circuit' (Shigenori 1992, p. 62)

The circuit of coenesthesis, like the external sensory-motor circuit, belongs to ordinary consciousness, but the experience of the coenesthesis circuit is more difficult to describe beyond terms like 'awareness of one's body' (ibid p. 62). We should note that memory and habituation are features of coenesthesis. We unconsciously and automatically mobilize body movements and positions without 'thinking.' There is thus a 'memory' system beneath conscious memory. As Shigenori puts it *"the body* learns and knows' (ibid p. 63, italics in original). We will give clinical examples that bear on this issue.

Yuasa's third organizational level is the **emotion-instinct circuit** (ibid, p. 63) which embraces those aspects of human functioning that have to do with sustaining vitality and life. It encompasses 'human instincts such as sexual desire and appetite' and the autonomic nervous system that controls and regulates the internal organs of the body. When this organizational system is out of balance we feel ill, stressed, or dis-eased. The activities of the internal organs governed by this system are largely independent of our will or intention, but they are very tied up with our emotional states.

The fourth level is the **unconscious quasi-body circuit**. This circuit raises the issue of experience that is unconscious, which is in some respects an oxymoron, depending on how we define consciousness, and how aware we are. We will see in chapter eleven, referring to Whitehead and Griffin's work, that we may speak of experience even in organisms that we do not usually understand as having our form of conscious experience. Be that as it may, the unconscious quasi-body circuit, in Yuasa's scheme, is below ordinary human consciousness, and unlike the first three circuits does not map onto ordinary anatomy. Its justification is the ki-meridian system of acupuncture medicine. It involves the flow of a type of energy, unique to living organisms:

***

To be more specific, when the flow of *ki* is examined psychologically, it can be perceived as an extraordinary sensation, as a lived-body's self-grasping sensation in a unique situation on the circuit of coenesthesis. (e.g., a case of a ki-sensitive person.) Furthermore, when it is seen physiologically, it can be detected on the surface of the skin which is a boundary wall between the body and the external world" (Yuasa 1986, p. 167). "In the case of a ki-sensitive person, ki-energy is said to be felt or intuited as a sensation of power from below the circuit of coenesthesis. ... In the light of the previous three circuits then, this unconscious quasi-body mediates between the first two circuits and the third emotion-instinct circuit. The first two circuits at least in part belong to "consciousness" and the third as Yuasa has noted has a close connection with the unconscious. Thus the unconscious quasi-body mediates between consciousness and the unconscious through the flow of ki-energy [Shigenori 1992, p. 71]

**

Having introduced Yuasa's circuits we are now in a position to experiment with applying them to meaning-*full* disease.

**

THE EXTERNAL SENSORY-MOTOR CIRCUIT

This circuit involves the recognition of stimuli from the external world by the sensory organs or modalities, such as vision or touch. This information is processed in the brain resulting in active motor responses such as moving the eyes or limbs. Yuasa's sensory-motor circuit is relevant to and active in both of Ichikawa's bodies, the object-body and subject body, in that we are aware of both subjective and objective aspects of the body when this circuit is activated.

For instance, let us consider patients with the very common condition of severe eczema of the skin. Allergy to foods or house dust mites may play an important role in eczema, but every allergist or dermatologist knows that many other factors are also important. One patient I am thinking of has severe eczema of face, arms and legs. There is a visual aspect to her problem. She *looks* at her arms and legs and *sees* disfiguring inflammation. She *hates* the appearance of her skin, and *wears* long-sleeved shirts and trousers to conceal it. Other sensory modalities, apart from vision, are involved as well. She *feels* intensely itchy, and *scratches* herself until she bleeds, and even then *persists* with scratching. There is a sensory stimulus both in the visual unattractiveness of her skin, and in the persistent itchiness. There is a motor response in both the covering up and the scratching. So we do have a sensory-motor circuit. Clearly this circuit contributes in a major way to the *object*-body. In the stimulus aspect she looks at the skin and sees it as ugly, and she feels itchy; in the motor aspect she covers it up and scratches it, as an object to be covered or scratched. She can, as it were, 'measure' the area. She can tell me exactly where the rash is and how big the affected area is, if I wished to know that. Thus we can see that the *sensory-motor circuit* and the *object-body* do map onto one another fairly well. It is a conceptualization that works to certain degree. If we can settle the inflammation her skin will be less ugly and less itchy and she will be free to uncover and scratch less. Many physicians would think like that.

But this is all too simple. It is true that we can perceive and isolate the patterns of the sensory-motor circuit within the complexity of her eczema, but we can hardly justify ignoring other elements. For example, her *hatred* of her appearance cannot be contained within a simple sensory stimulus/motor response circuit explanation. And while it may be tempting to reduce some diseases (including mild eczema) to a sensory-motor circuit and object-body construction, it certainly does not work very well in severe eczema.

I have had a number of patients with severe eczema who had previously been ineffectively treated using standard medical approaches, including various steroid and non-steroid skin creams, ultra-violet light irradiation, and a variety of oral drugs ranging from antihistamines with minimal side-effects to rather potent immunosuppressive drugs with some rather nasty side-effects. These treatments are all geared to reduce inflammation, which is the basis of the visual and itch stimuli we have been considering. We can say that these patients have been unsuccessfully treated from the perspectives of the object-body, and the sensory-somatic circuit. In case that appears unduly critical, I hasten to say that very severe eczema is often a very difficult management problem, and such treatments may be very useful.

Nevertheless, eczema can be looked at from a perspective hardly contemplated within the confines of a sensory-somatic circuit and object-body approach. In fact, we now treat most of these patients with a combination of allergy approaches and short-term psychotherapy because we find that the skin of eczema patients carries major meanings and the eczema settles much better if these are dealt with. We observe some interesting things in our work with these patients. Some of them continue to want to scratch even after their rash and itch has subsided. Recently, two such patients, with severe eczema that had settled very well with our combined allergy and mindbody approach, have continued to scratch vigorously, even though the itch has subsided. Both have said to me: "I *like* scratching!" There appears to be a habit pattern, and a comfort, even a conditioning towards scratching, that is not explained easily on a sensory stimulus and motor response circuit. I do not want to make this too complicated at this point, but there are many other possibilities why people may continue scratching. For example, many writers in the psychotherapy literature refer to self-stimulus and self-harm as a way of fostering a sense of aliveness.

In summary we have to say that, though it is possible to conceptualize many aspects of eczema within the sensory-somatic circuit, it is clearly underpinned by other circuits. I will give one example:

***

A woman in her twenties presents with severe eczema, particularly of her hands, which are severely inflamed, cracked, bleeding, and unresponsive to steroid creams. She has two infant children born eleven months apart and finds managing their bathing, nappy-changing, and dressing very difficult. The eczema had got dramatically worse following the birth of the second child. She does have some allergies, particularly to house dust mite, and her hands get very itchy in contact with house dust. We decided to try desensitizing her to the house dust mite, but some weeks into the treatment she pressured me for some better answers. We talked together about her life, and she disclosed that she had been the eldest child in a large family, and that she had had to carry a lot of responsibility because her mother was often ill. A key current issue for her in adult life and at the time her eczema worsened was that her husband was frequently away from home due to his work. In a dramatic unselfconscious gesture she lifted her hands in the air and exclaimed: 'And he leaves me carrying everything!' I was struck by this and said: "Look at your hands: Carrying everything and covered with eczema!' She laughed and then nodded. She went on to do thirteen sessions with a psychotherapist, and her hands settled. I continued the allergy desensitisation process, but both she and I felt that the most important intervention had been around dealing with her issues of carrying everything, and the way this issue had been repeated in her relationship with her husband, and stirred up by the arrival of her children.

***

While it is possible to conceptualize aspects of eczema within the framework of the sensory-somatic circuit of experience, there are other aspects of eczema that do not map onto this circuit.

The Circuit of Coenesthesis

As mentioned already, the experience of the circuit of coenesthesis belongs within ordinary consciousness, but it is more difficult to describe beyond rather vague terms such as 'awareness of one's body' (Shigenori 1992, p. 62). This is because it operates at the more 'hazy' end of conscious awareness, at least for the average person. In addition, this circuit has a kind of memory and a capacity for habituation. We see this aspect in operation when we stop to consider how we unconsciously and automatically mobilize body movements and positions without 'thinking.' From this it is said that "*the body* learns and knows' (ibid, p. 63). There are fairly obvious examples of this, such as the lightning-quick reactions involved in sporting activities.

An example of the interesting phenomenon of 'body memory' is that of classical conditioned or learned responses. There have been many reports of this phenomenon, but one example (Russell et al. 1984) involved guinea pigs rendered experimentally allergic to a protein. In subsequent experiments the allergic guinea pigs were fed with the protein, and at the same time their cages were flushed with a novel smell, thus pairing the onset of the allergic reaction with the exposure to the novel smell. The animals were treated so that they survived the consequent allergic reaction to the protein, then were rested for two weeks, and then re-exposed to the novel smell without exposure to the protein. They developed allergic reactions again. The body seemed to remember to react in the same way as when the protein was given. A powerful experience of allergy is remembered and reiterated even though the stimulus (cow protein) the immune system depends upon for the reaction is absent.

I have seen something similar in humans, particularly in people who have multiple drug reactions, but the most dramatic case involved a woman who nearly died due to bee venom allergy.

***

The patient was stung standing near a certain bee-hive and very nearly died from respiratory arrest. I desensitized her with graduated bee venom injections, a very well-attested scientific procedure that results in a virtually one hundred per cent cure rate. At the end of therapy, despite the fact she was receiving the equivalent of two bee-stings per injection, she remained understandably rather nervous about having a *live* bee sting. To help her with this I stung her with two *live* bees in my clinic, and she did not develop any adverse reaction. We went our different ways with a sense of mutual satisfaction. The next day, in complete confidence, she went out to the locality of the same hive where she had had the original near-catastrophic reaction. She got stung again, and developed an anaphylactic reaction, fortunately not as severe as the first.

***

Again, there is no orthodox immunological explanation for this. It is as if the 'body,' in both the guinea pigs and the patient, at some level, had memory of the original reaction, a memory that could be triggered again by the right set of circumstances, apparently independent of whether the allergen causing the reaction was present, or whether the bee venom-allergic patient was still allergic in immune terms. In the case of the guinea pigs, it is the conjunction of a serious reaction in the body and a novel smell. In the case of the patient, it is the conjunction of a sting, a sting in the right context, and the experience of a previous severe reaction in that context. Certainly it appears that the body or the person had 'learned.' Could we say that the body learned and knew? Specifically it appears that the organs associated with allergic responses were able to be re-activated given comparable circumstances.

Yuasa's circuit of coenesthesis emphasizes an aspect of human subject-body functioning hardly recognized at all in the management of disease. We have this capacity to 'remember' complex bodily patterns in response to very specific environmental stimuli.

I do recognize that behavioral psychologists would likely analyze these examples in terms of conditioned and unconditioned stimuli, and that would be a valid approach at a certain level, but it would not provide us with an in-depth understanding of underlying mechanism.

I am using the two examples to illustrate the organization of illness and disease in terms of *experience*, and am making no attempt to describe all the other possible narratives and mechanisms involved. At the risk of being tiresome, when one has a view of the organism as a unified but multidimensional whole, there are multiple narratives for what is happening in any one disease. In these two examples, we have (at least) the object-body narrative of histamine release (causing the measurable physical phenomena of anaphylaxis), the behaviorist narrative of learning, and the subject-body narrative focused around powerful experience and the implications for the body thereafter.

But we cannot so easily slide past the question as to whether these two examples are really types of meaning-*full* disease. Can we really construe guinea pig reactions as meaning-*full*? Are they merely (sic) *conditioned* reactions developing around what was for both animal and human a very uncomfortable experience, and which in both cases was also a threat to life. I am not sure these distinctions matter a lot. I guess it depends upon how we see *meaning* and *meaning-fullness*. When is a meaning a meaning? I was giving a workshop on mindbody approaches to physical disease recently. As a way of lightly winding-up the workshop the chairman told a story about his poodle, which he had left with his daughter whilst he traveled in Europe for six weeks. Soon after his departure the dog developed a troublesome eczema, which cleared when he returned. Many veterinarians would have little problem with idea that animals fret, or that their physical illnesses have a psychosomatic element. Most of us would have little hesitation in accepting that the dog 'missed' its owner. That 'feels' meaning-*full*, or at least experience-*full*. Undoubtedly this meaning is being experienced in a much more 'visceral' and non-cognitive way than we humans experience missing a loved one, but I suspect our experience and that of the poodle share the same meaning-*full* primitive core ingredients. I believe that much of the meaning in meaning-*full* disease ultimately rests on very important core experiences related to fundamental aspects of life, such as survival and threats to survival, relationship and threat to relationships. These core issues are shared by animals and humans alike, though they clearly become more nuanced, languaged, and thought about, as we climb the evolutionary tree, and as we grow from infancy to adulthood. An example may help.

***

A couple were referred because of marital difficulty. The husband was very controlling and unable to let his wife be free to be herself or to make independent decisions. In the course of the first session he complained of back-pain, and I enquired further about this. He had been previously diagnosed with ankylosing spondylitis, which is an inflammatory arthritis of the vertebral column leading, eventually, to a rigid fusion of all the vertebrae. Asked when the problem began, without any hesitation he gave the following intriguing story. Seven years before he had been present at his wife's first labour, during which an epidural anesthetic was given. He was absolutely appalled at the sight of the needle being inserted into his wife's spinal column, and collapsed in a faint on to the floor. He woke up with pain in his back, and had been 'feeling her pain' ever since. It is known that a certain genetic profile predisposes a person to ankylosing spondylitis, but the triggers for onset are unknown.

***

The first point I want to make here is that we see the same theme in all parts of the story. The man and his wife have what therapists call separation/individuation problems. He cannot see her as separate from himself, to the extent that he is excessively involved in all her decision-making, and is very controlling. We see a similar pattern as his wife gives birth. Unable to separate himself in a healthy way from what is happening to her, he collapses, wakes with back pain, and articulates it unself-consciously as 'feeling her pain.' There is an inadequate separation or boundary between them.

The second point is that this rather 'ordinary' issue of separation/individuation is likely rooted and grounded in much more primitive issues. Where does such failed separation/individuation and need to control come from? It may emerge from many varied elements. If we consider the trajectory of the human being from foetus to infant, to toddler, to school-age child, to teenager, and to adult, we recognize separation/individuation is a central element. Our first step is to separate from mother and be born, and at every stage more separation/individuation is achieved. But progress can be seriously distorted. For instance, every therapist knows that threats to survival or the integrity of the parent-child relationship can seriously affect a person's separation/individuation. If the infant has had a serious illness, or a close call with cot death, or the mother has lost a child previously, then fears and dreads may well lead to over-protectiveness, or inability to let go. The person may emerge into adulthood with distorted separation/individuation patterns. These may manifest in various ways including the fusional behaviors we discern in the story above. In other words, the meanings identifiable around the epidural anesthetic, and the lack of marital freedom, and the pain carried by the man, all likely rest on much more primitive issues such as threat to survival or relationship. It is probably valid anyway to say that threat to relationship is ultimately a threat to survival.

Returning then to the guinea pigs and the bee sting allergic woman we might assume that the meaning in these cases is something to do with the experience of threat to survival of the *subject-body*, and a learned or body memory pattern in relation to this. Because the object-body (were it to exist as an isolated entity) has no subjectivity it cannot learn in response to such threat.

It might seem that these are all very unusual examples, and not of general significance. But let's consider the important phenomenon called Chronic Fatigue Syndrome. Many patients with this 'condition' have consulted me over the years. Some of them have come believing they have a food allergy responsible for the symptoms, others have been referred by general practitioners knowing my mindbody approach to disease, and others come because it is assumed that the condition may have an immune basis. Patients complain of a variety of symptoms, at the centre of which is a profound feeling of fatigue and depletion, or lack of energy to do ordinary activities, or a collapse into prolonged exhaustion after ordinary effort. They may also complain of a wide variety of physical symptoms including aches and pains suggestive of 'fibromyalgia,' abdominal symptoms suggestive of 'irritable bowel syndrome,' problems with skin temperature regulation, and so on. Ordinary blood tests reveal little evidence of inflammation despite attempts by many researchers to sheet this problem home to a 'physical' cause.

There is a common pattern of Chronic Fatigue Syndrome (CFS) that is of real interest in relation to Yasua's body schema, and I will describe this pattern in terms of *predisposing, precipitating,* and *perpetuating* factors. CFS is frequently triggered or *precipitated* by a viral infection, such as influenza or infectious mononucleosis (glandular fever), though other non-infectious trigger factors include an unusual stress event such as an excessive work-load, or even some relatively minor life event on top of a sustained background pressure.

Staying with a virus-triggered example, a typical patient develops symptoms of infection including aches and pains, fatigue, as well as other symptoms usually seen with an active virus infection such as sore throat, blood count changes, fever, catarrh, and cough, the variations depending on the type of virus involved. As the virus clears these latter symptoms disappear, but our typical chronic fatigue patient is left with the fatigue and aches and pains. The patient's symptoms fluctuate, but most complain that no matter what the level of improvement they do not return to their expected 'normal.' A variety of triggers may tip them back into the symptom pattern: Undue effort, lack of sleep, a stressful encounter, another viral infection, and so on. These are the *perpetuating* factors. Some of these patients get a return of the full 'bag' of symptoms that occurred at the beginning of the illness, as if the viral illness has returned. In the vast majority of such patients there is no evidence of this at a laboratory investigation level.

How should we interpret this pattern of endless reiteration of virus-induced symptoms when the virus is gone? It appears to me, phenomenologically, that the body falls back into a body symptom pattern that it 'learned' during the initial illness. This is rather similar to the guinea pigs and the bee allergy woman who 'learned' anaphylaxis. Yasua's coenesthetic circuit with its memory at the hazy end of consciousness may provide a model for understanding such 'memory.'

There are Western researchers approaching the same issues. In his classic paper, *The Body Keeps the Score,* Van der Kolk (1994) describes how, under stressful conditions, traumatized people 'feel, or act as if they were traumatised all over again. Thus, high states of arousal seem to selectively promote retrieval of traumatic memories, sensory, information, or behaviors associated with prior traumatic

experience.' A pattern, or schema of symptoms that developed originally in relation to the initiating event, is constantly revived in the
same form by cues from the environment or under stress. This is
similar to what we see in CFS.

Van der Kolk's work is focused around patients who have suffered massive psychological trauma such as sexual abuse, war experience, and torture. Traumatized people react in multiple ways, and
two of these are clearly relevant to meaning-*full* disease. They *dissociate*, that is, they split off the memory from ordinary consciousness
so its painful quality does not surface. And they *somatize*, that is they
express the 'emotional' intensity of the trauma in a bodily symptom,
without experiencing the subjective emotional aspect. Many of these
patients repeatedly express their trauma in stereotypical physical
pattern. While many of my patients with meaning-*full* disease do
not have histories of *massive* trauma some do so, and many do have
life stories which can be understood as damaging, or deprived, or
emotionally ambiguous or impoverished, or repeatedly injurious in
a less massive way.

Returning now to patients with Chronic Fatigue Syndrome we
could ask whether they are actually re-enacting the physical event
in their bodies or 'remembering' the symptoms, in a re-stimulated
way, in response to certain cues? It seems as if it is more the latter
because laboratory investigation shows little evidence of a major
recurrence of infection. In contrast, there is no doubt that the
'remembered' anaphylaxis, in the guinea pigs and the bee venom
allergy woman, were actual physical events, not just (sic) memories. All of this leaves one musing as to the basis for *chronic* disease
of all kinds.

But CFS cannot be reduced merely to a 'remembered' symptom
pattern based on the memory capacity of the coenesthetic circuit. We
find that certain people are *predisposed* to the development of CFS,
following a viral infection. They are people with rather typical
themes in their lives. They are often hard-working, excessively
responsible, high-performing, and greatly appreciated for their contributions to society. As a consequence they may feel over-loaded,
used by employers and family, and that there is little space for getting their own needs met. They are often people who want to please,
are afraid of conflict, and out of touch with their own negative feelings, let alone able to express them directly. Often the viral infection

arrives at a time when the whole structure of their lives is precariously poised, and over they go. The way they have structured their lives has become a liability, and it cannot be sustained. Some will struggle back to near-normal functioning. Some will take a long time out and gradually their lives will become re-structured around a much reduced level of functioning. Others will start to look deeply into the structure of their lives and start doing it all rather differently, gradually achieving a degree of health that is not dependent on going back to the old treadmill.

If this is so, how do we relate it to coenesthetic circuit memory? I believe the *pattern* of the symptoms is related to the initiating event, the infection. The infection creates the symptom structure. But that event is nested within a wider context of life-world meaning for that patient. It is exhausting to be in the world meeting impossible demands without due care for one's own needs. The infection collapses the whole structure and sets up a memory pattern for the body around which all these themes of meaning cluster.

This brings us back again to the *perpetuating* factors. I return now to the case of John (presented earlier in this chapter) whose illness was not triggered by a virus but whose predisposing story was very much that described above.

***

John is aged thirty-nine, and was a valued administrator in a financial services business where growth had been phenomenal, and staffing had not kept up with the work-load increases. He took on more and more responsibility and became progressively exhausted. His wife said of him that 'he can never say "no!"' Apparently this was a long-standing pattern, seen in all aspects of his life. Eventually an unexplained episode of deafness in one ear took him to his doctor, who was unable to provide a satisfactory explanation. He returned to work, and suddenly collapsed. He described the sensation as an 'incredible heaviness'; and 'it was like my spine was collapsing, shrinking down until it was only two inches long.' He was conscious during this first event, but unable to move his limbs, which he described as 'paralysed and heavy.' When he recovered from the paralysis the deafness had gone. He had intensive neurological investigations but no definitive diagnosis was made, and three years later, at the time of consultation with me, was chronically fatigued, unable to work, and was having three to four collapse episodes a day, all rather similar to the original collapse. He hesitated to leave the house and frequently got collapse episodes when left alone. He was confined to home doing gardening, which he enjoyed greatly. He was very angry that the medical profession was dismissive of his symptoms, because he did not fit into their usual diagnostic classification systems and because they were powerless to help him.

***

What are the perpetuating factors here? We can guess at them because they are always popping up in these situations in different variations: Lack of a diagnosis; fear of something serious being missed, of the unknown, and of the future; negative interactions with the medical profession; frustration at being so constrained; relief at not having to go back into the world and take on all the burdens again; an ongoing background reward from people attending to his needs; and legitimation of his own identity—he can do his gardening at home without feeling guilt for being self-centered. During the course of five sessions, as these factors were discussed and resolved, he got a complete remission of his symptoms and resumed normal activities.

There seems to be a 'remembered' pattern of fatigue and collapse symptoms rooted in something like the coenesthetic circuit level of organization, and emerging in the context of prior vulnerabilities and contextual perpetuating factors. And, certainly, the collapse metaphor is vividly expressive of the crushing experience of his work. Invoking the subject-body seems much more appropriate here than the object-body.

But there may be even more to this syndrome of chronic fatigue. I want to consider Yuasa's third and fourth organizational levels, the emotion-instinct circuit, and the unconscious quasi-body circuit, together. The former embraces those aspects of human functioning that have to do with sustaining vitality and life. It encompasses 'human instincts such as sexual desire and appetite' and the autonomic nervous system that controls and regulates the internal organs of the body. So this circuit maps onto the control and balancing mechanisms of the autonomic nervous system and endocrine system of the object-body, which maintain life and vitality through mechanisms that we are neither conscious of or, normally, have any control over. When this organizational system is out of balance we feel ill, stressed, or dis-eased. The activities of the internal organs governed by this system are largely independent of our will or intention, but they are very tied up with our emotional states. The **unconscious quasi-body circuit** involves a flow of a type of energy unique to living organisms.

I do not have the theoretical authority in this area to put forward more than a few ideas, but I have seen many patients with CFS and want to write from that experience. I have listened very carefully to their exact language, to *their* subjective phenomenology. What do they say? They complain of an unpleasant fatigue, of utter depletion, of inability to do, of lack of the resources necessary to enact an intention, of starting something and then being deeply aware of the impossibility of going on, of not being able to raise the energy required, of attempting the smallest thing and feeling profoundly depleted, of suddenly caving in and slipping to an exhausted prostrated place, and so it goes on. It is like the inner springs of energy have been turned off, or have dwindled to a trickle. It is like organs previously sustained with enough power and energy now groan and grumble with lack of vitality. We talk about being energized; these people are de-energised. What's more, they are profoundly troubled by it. It has a deeply felt quality. It feels 'awful.' It is not like the tiredness of a day's hard physical work. They feel hardly alive. They want it to be different. It is a painful, awful place to know one's self as alive, but not feel properly alive. And what makes it worse is that many in the medical profession react negatively to the condition because we cannot find a laboratory test to legitimate it as a real disease under the rubric of the Western biomedical model.

Let's consider it from Yuasa's emotion-instinct and unconscious quasi-body circuits. I wonder if CFS represents some sort of stifling, or cut-off, or strangling, or limitation of vital energy flow and/or balance? In biomedicine we do have some important things to say about energy *levels*. We know that psychological things like attitude, mood, relational support are important to motivation and energy. We know that biomedical things such as hormone levels influence us profoundly. But we have little to say about the *vital* difference between a living and a non-living organism. Such things get a little close to old ideas of *vitalism* and spirituality for the comfort of Western materialists. I believe we must consider the possibility that the (subject-) body has a fundamental vitality, spirit, and energy which can under certain circumstances be stifled or dysfunctional.

In summary, Yasua's schemata provide at least a provocative pilot model for thinking about the construction of body organization according to *experience*, particularly in some diseases such as CFS. I have chosen to map this syndrome onto the coenesthetic, emotion-instinct, and unconscious quasi-body circuits merely because it is a poorly understood condition and because it has elements that illustrate a possible utility for this experience-based scheme. I would assume though that if it is truly relevant to CFS then it will be relevant to many other conditions.

CHAPTER TWELVE

Experience as a 'fundamental'

D isease is both a disturbance of the physical and an expression of 'experience.' If we have 'eyes' to see and 'ears' to hear, experience, and its associated meanings, can be discerned simultaneously in both the speech and the physical diseases of patients. The congruence can be vivid.

***

At age 44 Valerie had a hysterectomy for fibroids, and about the same time she developed a condition called lichen sclerosus, an unpleasant inflammatory condition of the genitals, which leads to scarring and discomfort (amongst other symptoms). Again about the same time as the lichen sclerosus began, she stopped having a sexual relationship with her husband because her sexual relationship with him was emotionally aversive, and because sex 'no longer had any meaning' for her. Later she developed bladder inflammation (cystitis) as well. It became very clear that the marriage had long been unsatisfactory, and much of her anger and frustration stemmed from unresolved emotions relating to her husband's affair 18 years before, to his emotional inaccessibility, and to her inability to mobilize other options like marital counseling or leaving the marriage. I saw the inflammation of the genital and bladder areas as metaphorically expressing her anger, and her need to distance herself from her husband whilst keeping the relationship overtly stable and satisfactory.

***

In this narrative, Valerie's experience and her disease mirror one another. The body, relationship, experience, and disease are all entangled. But it is one thing to show these entangled relationships from a phenomenological perspective, and it is quite another to explain them in a more fundamental way. Many of us do find it intuitively reasonable to accept the reality of a relationship between experience and disease, and the descriptive categories of subject-body and object-body are helpful in making some sense of the issues. But none of this really tells us what the relationship between experience and the physical is at depth.

One of the problems is how we should define experience. This proves to be very difficult, the main reason being that our capacity for experience, or the fact that we do experience anything, remains a mystery, and this is not solved by finding more and more words to describe *aspects* of our experiences. We know we experience, and we know experience has many aspects, but grasping an 'essence' of experience is much more problematic. Psychotherapists try and capture experience within the categories of feelings, or emotions. There are other categories that are often identified with experience, such as awareness, perception, intuition, and states of consciousness, but for various reasons none of these capture all aspects of experience either. The problem is partly the very process of categorization. Categorization, by its very nature, is always an action, by a languaged observer, of dividing the 'whole' into bits or fragments. Thus, the above-mentioned categories, and any others, can never capture the whole. Mysteries are often better captured by stories and parables than by definitions.

Therefore, I will resort to using the word 'experience' *itself* as my basic term, and try and make it clear when I am talking about a certain aspect of experience. In general, *experience* is being used here in the sense of that which arises from a capacity for *living awareness and responsiveness*. At some level variants of this capacity are present in all organized living systems, and they become increasingly sophisticated as we move up the evolutionary ladder. Most of the categories of experience I have already mentioned above are those we identify as human, but I assume here that all other animal species have a capacity for experience *at their own level*.

It is important to emphasise that experience, flowing out of a capacity for *living awareness and responsiveness*, is not a category separate from the organism's bodily nature, nor from the organism's environmental context. Experience is intimately tied up with the fact that we are somatic and physical. *We cannot divide experience from the body just as we cannot divide the mind from the body.* This takes us back again to the modern concept of embodiment, that we are *embodied*, or, as I prefer it, *bodied*. *Embodiment* represents a conceptual attempt to get away from the idea rooted in Cartesian thinking that our experience, mind, or consciousness is somehow independent of the body, and also a widespread modern academic movement to bring mind and experience back together with the body. It attempts to re-integrate these aspects with our body, with the attendant risk of reducing all of them *to* body, as if they are *only* body.

Experience, and the capacity for it, is not something added to a 'dead matter' organism. Rather, it flows out of the very nature of the organism. Leder (1992) emphasises that modern medicine has been built upon a 'dead body' view of the person. In contrast, the reality is captured by the much more dynamic notion of the *lived body*. This *lived body* terminology emphasises two things. The first is captured by the notion of *embodiment*. There is no experience or awareness that is not intimately tied up with, constructed by, *in some way* embodied in, or mediated through our physical makeup. We are incarnate beings. I do not thereby exclude experiences that may have their *origin* in un-embodied reality, but I assume that such hypothetical realities get mediated to us in ways that *always include* our bodies.

The *lived body* terminology also emphasises that the unified, unitary, experiencing body lives in a context, in an environment, in the world. There is no individual experiencing body without a world that impacts it, and which it impacts in a complex ongoing fashion. The body experiences *in* a world. It is thus sheer nonsense to treat the body as if it is a highly individualized, separate, isolated mechanism. Acting *as if* it is so, at least temporarily, may have its uses, for instance in some surgical procedures, but for many chronic illnesses it is totally inadequate. When patients fill our clinics with asthma, diabetes, back pain, eczema, and when our gaze is confined to the individualized mechanistic body we are guilty of ignoring much of reality. Valerie's diagnosis of lichen sclerosus with the painful, atrophied genitalia makes so much sense when we know about her 'painful,' 'angry,' 'atrophied' marital relationship. Can we legitimately ignore the possibility that the *physical* body may be behaving the way it is because of the patient's subjective experience which we have rendered invisible? Can we ignore the possibility that her *experiencing* body may be manifesting the way it is because it is in lively reciprocal contact with a rich context that includes husband, family, culture, and society?

Thus we have 'experience' which emerges from an embodied capacity for living awareness and responsiveness within, and in interaction with, a rich multifaceted environment. This is the context for this chapter, which explores the nature of 'experience' and its relationship to meaning-*full* disease.

Most psychotherapists focus on experience as projected into expressed feelings and emotions because these are aspects of experience that the psychotherapy model of therapy works with. Feelings and emotions *are* aspects of experience, but do not capture the whole of experience. For instance, we actually experience, or are aware of, our stream of conscious thought in a way that is different to a computer. We assume the latter does not *experience* its stream of informational processing. The flow of information in conscious thought is not easily explained in terms of the feelings, emotions, or affects favored by psychotherapists. *Awareness* may be a better term for this aspect of experience. We are aware of being alive, of thinking actively, and of having choice and options as we experience this stream of conscious thought. I am, of course, making no distinction at this point between awareness and self-awareness. I am assuming that the latter is a complex (mainly human) variant of general awareness. It looks then as if the capacity for experience is not just simply a capacity for feelings like joy, happiness, hate, anger, fear, guilt, shame and all the other feelings that therapists work with. Awareness of our stream of thought or consciousness is also part of experience whether it is clearly tinged with feeling or emotion or not.

While psychotherapists tend to relate human experience to feelings, it is likely that there is a capacity in nature for experience that is more fundamental than the sophisticated human capacity for feelings. I assume that amoebae do not have feelings in the way we understand feelings, but they do respond to their environment. Philosophers have attempted to capture the generic elements of experience. Nagel (1974) actually defines experience *as something it is like*. Think of when you were last asked about a particular experience. You are likely to have replied that 'it was *like* … this or that.' For example, suppose I am asked what it was *like* to have a motor vehicle accident, and remain pinned under the car for an hour. As I tell you what *it was like*, I draw on feelings of fear (of dying), my bodily sensations of pain or numbness, my thought patterns around possible loss of relationship with my family, my sense of helplessness and powerlessness, my sagging hope that I will eventually be noticed by someone, and many other things. These are all aspects of my experiencing, and my capacity for experience. But they are *aspects* of this strange and wonderful capacity to be aware of what *it is like*.

Griffin (1998), to whom we will turn later in the chapter, addresses the capacity for experience in another way. He talks about our physicality, and that of the world, as the *outside*, and of experience as the *inside*. "Experience is not what we are for others but what we are *for ourselves*" (ibid, p. 65). Because experience is our internal experience of ourselves we only ever have the option of saying what *it is like* because no one else can see it, hear it, touch it, or smell it. I can only tell you what it is *like* on the *inside*. This approach to experience is reminiscent of the phenomenological perspective, that we are both *object-bodies* (the outside) and *subject-bodies* (the inside).

Experience is then this curious capacity we have on the inside to be aware of what it is like. It is a capacity fundamental to feeling, emotion, affect, and bodily states, as well as fundamental to being *aware* of my thinking and stream of consciousness. Experience is fundamental to being alive, and maybe the capacity for experience is one of the crucial elements of being alive. We might hesitate at this notion, but when we return to Griffin (vide infra) we will see that he argues that all forms of life have a capacity for experience in some form, though of course not necessarily at the level we would regard as consciousness.

I have been setting the stage conceptually. Let's now ground our exploration of experience by looking at two very interesting disease stories, which seemed to arise in the context of 'experience' of sexual abuse. I presented the first case in chapter one but the story bears repetition here as an important foil to the second case.

***

Margaret, age 44, was referred for depression triggered when she was embraced by her church minister who was clearly sexually aroused. When aged 15, her twin brother sexually assaulted her, beginning with a demand that she expose her breasts, and going on to forceful vaginal penetration. She was left bleeding and traumatized. During therapy we uncovered almost unutterable feelings in relation to this trauma, and collaterally she developed excessive bleeding from the uterus. She was thoroughly investigated by a gynecologist, and eventually had a hysterectomy. Within a few weeks she started to pass blood in her urine. Despite further investigation by a urologist the source of this bleeding was never found, and she continued to periodically pass blood in the urine, especially at times when she felt badly treated by powerful males (in her financial-services work-place). But this was not the end of the phenomena. She then developed bleeding from both her breasts. Again she was thoroughly investigated and nothing sinister was found. Margaret and I realized from early on that the bleeding from the breasts commenced at the time we were exploring her feelings towards her brother who raped her.

***

The crucial element for us here is that the original traumatic rape 'experience' had vivid physical and subjective elements, and these were being echoed in her presentation nearly three decades later. There were powerful and, at times, quite unmanageable negative subjective elements including powerlessness, loneliness, fragmentation, fear, and rage. At the same time there were the vivid physical experiences of bleeding from the genital and urinary tracts, and the breasts. The physical breast, genital, and urinary tract phenomena, and the subjective feelings, are all part of the whole rape experience. The 'experience' is both subjective and physical at one and the same time. And, despite the passage of many years Margaret's subject-body seemed once again able to represent the 'experience' very accurately in much the same form as occurred in the rape. Experience and physical disability, dysfunction, and disease are deeply present together.

I want to emphasize two elements in Margaret's story. Firstly, there is the intense relationship between experience and body manifestation. Secondly, she appears to carry the experience and its consequences as an *individual*. This raises an important issue. Should we assume that the relationship between experience and disease is an individual matter? Certainly, apart from genetic disorders, this is how we tend to think in the individualistic West. But, as we have seen, experience is always something that emerges in a context, and within relationships, and it becomes conceivable that some diseases may actually represent *someone else's* experience.

***

Kelly, age six, was referred for immunological assessment for severe inflammation of her genitals (a condition called vulvitis) unresponsive to antifungal and steroid creams, and of two years duration. She would wake her mother up five times nightly distressed by the irritation. Routine enquiry as to whether she may have been sexually abused uncovered the mother's own sexual abuse, which had never previously been disclosed to a health professional. It turned out that the mother had prevented the child from being on her own with males, and had also been emotionally over-involved with the child in a variety of other ways. Early in the consultation I noticed that the child seemed unusually attuned to mother. I suggested to mother that the problem was really hers, relating to her own sexual abuse. I told the child that from now on mother was not going to worry about her. I instructed mother to under-respond to the girl's symptoms and to keep a symptom graph so as to divert her concern and anxiety away from her relationship with the child, and onto the graph paper. She was never to ask about her symptoms but to graph unsolicited symptoms reported by the girl. The child was given soothing creams to apply herself, without mother's help, and instructed to ask for a bath if she was sore. Mother was asked to pour the bath, but to avoid all other interest or involvement. She was to give much love and attention but only at times when the child was not complaining of symptoms. Three weeks later they returned for follow-up and reported that the child's symptoms settled within a day of the assessment. Mother entered psychotherapy for resolution of her own abuse issues. The child's symptoms remained resolved.

***

A member of a family is ill because of another family member's experience? Is this going too far? In respect of our focus here, this phenomenon fits very well with the concept of the *lived body*, which recognizes that a person is far from an isolated atom, or an island. In the West we have emphasized individuality, and the separateness of bodies, to the point that we can hardly imagine disease as arising from disordered relationships, let alone as an expression of someone else's experience.

What we forget is that our individuality is really a semi-stable reality, very subject to change, and it often takes much energy to achieve and maintain. It emerges within a complex cauldron of influences which are always shaping us both towards individuality and towards the communal. Individuality is always in relation to the communal. This is focused up sharply when we think of intimacy. Good intimate relationship is always a living ongoing tension between being truly myself, and being capable of being close with others. As I write I think of a case just seen in my clinic.

***

Helen, aged 48, has progressively worsening itchy rash (urticaria) for thirty years, abdominal pain for fifteen years, and severe eye and nose inflammation for five years. She has been intensively investigated by numerous other specialists. There was no evidence of allergy, but what I did hear in her language was a recurrent reference to 'mother.' When asked about when her various symptoms began, worsened, or improved, she responded by referring to times when this or that happened to either her mother or her mother-in-law. This was my first clue to the recurring motifs of her experience. It gradually became clear that she was highly enmeshed with her mother, who was a demanding, guilt-inducing, manipulative person (who herself had had very traumatic mothering). Life was characterized by fluctuating, persistent, internal conflicts around both *remaining in relationship* with mother and *getting free to live her own life*. Her mother-in-law was, by contrast, the perfect mother. As the session went on both she and her husband were very clear that the fluctuations of her symptoms had paralleled the vicissitudes of her relationship with her mother. She could hardly imagine it ever being different.

***

This woman is not in a good intimate relationship with her mother. Unless she gets some healthy separateness and distance from her dysfunctional mother I predict she will remain unwell. The story underscores the idea that for healthy functioning we depend upon being both 'individual' and able to get in close with an 'other,' and, in that closeness, not being violated by the 'other.' If such closeness becomes problematic, or unsafe, and we do not have adequate defenses we can expect a stirring up of intense feelings, and often these will be expressed in the body, as in Helen's case.

Now let's return to Kelly's case which is more startling than that of Helen. She develops, by proxy, bodily symptoms that have to do with failure of intimate relations *between her mother and her mother's abuser*. Kelly experiences the protective male-avoidant attitudes and behaviours of her mother, and eventually manifests a disease that appears to be a powerful metaphorical representation of the things that she has absorbed from her mother. She seems to have a disease based on meanings communicated through the family system without the use of verbal symbolic language. Careful enquiry had convinced me that there had been no discussion whatsoever with the child about sexual matters or abuse. Indeed mother had been careful to avoid any disclosure of her own abuse to anybody prior to her interview with me. Even if in the unlikely event the mother had discussed the abuse with her six year old child we would still stand and wonder how the child could then have proceeded to represent such 'understanding' in inflamed genitals. Certainly the mother's abuse had profoundly affected her management of her daughter, who presumably experienced *something* relating to the abuse in her relationship with her mother, and she finally represents this experience in a vividly appropriate disease manifestation.

Children are frequently affected by the problematic experiences of other family members. As I write I recall two situations arising in my clinic recently:

***

The first family presented with an eight-year old boy with two years of persistent abdominal pain that had been intensively investigated. His sleep and schooling had been disrupted. Careful enquiry showed that it began when his sister was diagnosed with a malignancy, and the family was thrown into crisis.

My feeling was that the pain was a representation of several things including fear around what was happening in the family, need for attention for himself, and a continuing anxiety in the parents that he too might have something sinister that was undiagnosed. I framed the illness up in this way, explained the way emotions get communicated in all sorts of ways through families, told the child he was well and that I was not worried about him, and that his parents were not going to worry about him any longer, and asked the parents to give the child lots of love and attention *but only when he was not complaining of the pain.* Three weeks later he was free of pain, attending school consistently, sleeping well, and had been 'player of the day' in football.

***

The second family presented with a four year old boy with recurrent diarrhoea and lethargy developing over several months. Gradually the story emerged of the mother having developed a serious illness and requiring hospitalisation. Her confidence had been severely knocked and it had taken months for her to face life without being impaired by anxiety as to what might happen next, because her illness made her subject to future possible health emergencies, and they lived in a rural area far from medical help. One of her fears was that the boy might be potentially seriously ill as well. In the interview the father suggested rather cautiously that he thought the boy had not been right since his mother had been ill. I dealt with this situation in much the same way as with the first family, except that I offered to spend time with mother in the hope that she might develop a more settled perspective on her own illness and be able to see her son in a more separate way. They did not engage in further sessions.

***

Children pick up or 'experience' far more than we usually suspect, and they often convert the feelings they have around such experiences into bodily symptoms. In addition, these cases emphasize that life is indeed for us a continuum of rich experience, both as individuals and in community. We are all caught up in the experience of others. The experience of one individual may at times be powerfully projected or communicated into a surrounding community of individuals, and one member of that community may finally manifest that experience in illness or disease. In a sense the individual becomes the sign of a problem in the wider system. This idea is not new; family therapists have spoken of such things over recent decades though not so much in relation to physical disease.

One of the interesting points in Kelly's case was that the transmission of meaning was not via direct verbal dialogue between parent and child. This raises the important issue of the relationship between 'experience' and language, which turns out to be very relevant to meaning-*full* disease. Most of us who are not research psychologists or philosophers tend to conflate experience with thinking and language. As adults, our experience, thinking, and language have become so entangled that this conflation is completely understandable. But it is also problematic. To clarify this let's return again (see also chapter six) to human beings who have not yet developed verbal language.

Few people would doubt that the foetus and the infant are hosts to profound experience. We imagine that an infant experiences the warmth and comfort of its mother, or, conversely, the sense of being cut off from her. We quite naturally impose adult language structures upon these experiences. These language structures are really thought-based symbolic interpretations of the experience of the infant. We might observe approvingly: '*Look, she is asleep on her mother's breast, she's warm and cosy, and feels so safe, as if nothing in the world could disturb her; doesn't it warm your heart—ah, to be so trusting!*' As I reflect on such comments I am very aware of the complex processes of my thinking *about* the infant's experience. But the infant is experiencing the *essentials* of these experiences in some raw, perhaps primitive, but meaning-*full* form, *unmediated by thought and language*. Simply put, the infant is not thinking about them, she is experiencing them.

Whatever *our* needs are to have unifying categories for these experiences of love, warmth, and safety, so that we can converse about them, there is little doubt that talk about them is not central to the infant. The infant needs *the experiences themselves*, of being loved, comforted, reassured, and kept safe. And it seems that the infant has the capacity to experience these things long before the development of language.

I am saying therefore that 'experience' is prior to language, prior to the capacity we eventually develop to symbolize the experiences (of love, warmth, etc.) with thinking, images, language, and metaphors.

We have privileged the rich complexity and creativity of the (overlaid and derivative) language and thought elements to such an extent that the antecedent *raw experiences* generally have quite low status. Our 'hearts' can be stirred; we can have deep 'gut' experiences; and we recognize the raw, uncontrolled, primitive qualities of these. We yearn to be moved at these levels; yet we also fear the unmanageability of primordial experience. We learn to manage our primordial experiences with the sophisticated skills of thought and language, and we divert the associated energies into a welter of acceptable activities. But none of this gainsays our capacity for raw experience. Do we always manage this raw energy and capacity in effective ways? And how might any lack of effectiveness in such management relate to the emergence of meaning-*full* disease? For one thing, it is possible, even very likely, that we have residues, from infancy, of raw, primitive, and disturbed experience that are not well resolved or managed in the ordinary processes of languaged communication with important others. This raises then the question of how much physical disease is actually a bodily representation of unresolved pre-verbal experience that cannot be transmuted into language forms, or resolved in those forms.

Biomedicine would be scandalized by this idea that the origin of many diseases could in part originate in the primitive pre-verbal experience of infants. In chapter one I quoted from de Quincey concerning the

***

standard scientific view of nature ... that it is composed of "dead matter" – so that even living systems are ultimately composed of unfeeling, purposeless, meaningless atoms embedded in equally unfeeling, purposeless, and meaningless fields of force [de Quincey 2002].

***

Biomedicine is based on this standard scientific view. At rock-bottom, reality is devoid of experience. Experience is an epiphenomenon, a later development. Of course, biomedical clinicians might concede the possibility of early experience in the fetus and the infant, but because of their biological reductionism stance few would spend time imagining these experiences, and even less time pondering the possibility that those experiences could be playing a germinal role in the development of physical disease.

We see this 'dead matter' perspective expressed every day, for example in paediatric practice where a miserable six week old infant will be assessed for reflux oesophagitis, milk allergy, or colic, but little consideration will be given to what the child is 'experiencing' in a wider sense. Put brutally, within the biomedical framework the infant is a biological machine constructed from 'dead matter.' Paediatricians feel they have done their job if they have found nothing wrong with the machine and its parts. There are many kind paediatricians, but in the end the dead matter/machine model of the person underwrites most of their work.

The same assumptions cause adult physicians, who treat, for example, severe asthma, ulcerative colitis, or rheumatoid arthritis patients year after year with drugs, not infrequently with damaging side-effects, to laugh at the notion that their patients' symptoms might be rooted in possibly unutterable early experiences that have never been able to be languaged. Moreover, if these experiences could ever be languaged in meaning-*full* speech, the same assumptions of 'dead matter' would lead these physicians to declare such meanings irrelevant.

This way of doing medicine pivots on the assumption that matter is 'dead matter' devoid of experience, and though experience does develop it is a secondary element. Modern biomedicine has taken this assumption so far that for most clinicians it is inconceivable that 'experience' and meaning could be as constitutive of disease as are genetics and biochemistry.

But maybe there is change in the air. In a moment I will invoke the work of three modern philosophers, Alfred North Whitehead, David Chalmers, and David Ray Griffin, who have argued powerfully for the overthrow of 'dead matter' assumptions, and for recognising experience, or the capacity for experiencing, as being as fundamental as mass, energy, and time. This is a complex area but we do need to address it because, without creating a fundamental place for experience in our models, we cannot explain meaning-*full* disease phenomena, and without a good explanatory model it will be impossible for most clinicians to accept the need and responsibility to work with the experience and meanings aspects of physical diseases.

Let's return to the question of models, in particular the biomedical and biopsychosocial models. They rely ultimately upon two major assumptions, those of materialism and dualism. Taking the biomedical model first, it really is a deeply materialistic model in which all clinical reality is reduced to matter and mechanism. *Materialistic monism* is its philosophical position. By that we mean that reality is fundamentally, pervasively, and continuously material, and that is all. The mind is derivative, an epiphenomenon of matter, and, as such, is afforded scant regard from biomedical clinicians. In this model, because matter is fundamental, all aspects of disease will be most fundamentally grasped by understanding the purely physical elements of the dysfunction. When mind or 'experience' is considered, it is seen as arising from matter and ultimately reducible to matter. More than that, mind and 'experience' have been treated dualistically—that is, carved off from the body as a separate entity. The biomedical model is therefore monistic in the way it reduces everything to matter, but dualistic in the way it handles the mind.

The biopsychosocial model certainly honours the mind more. It shares many of the assumptions of the biomedical model, but the big difference is that it treats the mind as *important*, and not just as a mere bystander to the *real* physical origins of disease. Nevertheless, while it emphasises the influence of the mind on the body, the mind has until recently been largely treated as a separate entity.

All of this has significance for trying to understand the many meaning-*full* diseases I have presented thus far. In the two models, the meanings and experience we see represented in the physical symptoms of meaning-*full* disease must be assumed to be in some way generated in a mind that is separated off from the body. Remember the mind is assumed to be a carved off separate entity. And remember that this creates a very special set of problems when it comes to meaning-*full* disease. These meanings, generated apparently in a separate mind, must finally get expressed in a metaphorical disease in the body. To do this they must follow a certain pathway. Firstly, they need to be transmuted from mental states (in the separated-off mind) into brain states, and then, secondly, they must be projected out from the brain towards the metaphorically relevant body area. The question becomes whether such a sequence or pathway is actually plausible?

This is where Kelly's story is so pertinent. We have mother's experience of sexual abuse, and her protective behaviours towards Kelly. Mother has a lot in *her* mind regarding abuse. We have little idea of what Kelly had in *her* mind about this. Would there really be anything there that we as adults would recognize as an abuse 'story'? It is also really difficult to imagine that whatever it is which is in her mind (*has* to be in her mind according to these dualistic models) is then transmuted into some sort of brain state and then projected very accurately to her genitals. Surely the possibility arises that these dualistic models in which the separated mind is the repository for all meaning are just plain wrong. Maybe meaning is carried in different ways. We need to look for new possibilities and one of these may be that meaning and experience are much more inherently part of so-called 'dead matter.'

Taking this direction we can consider both Kelly and her mother as *living bodies*, a term which we have already seen implies a mutual interactional context deeply pervaded by personal, family, societal, and cultural meanings. A *living body* concept of person would assume that Kelly must be influenced in some way by her mother's sexual abuse. But the way in which it manifests is rather shocking. The somatic metaphor of her vulvitis, representing her mother's abuse, appears to violate 'reality.' Firstly, it seems to violate our understandings of the *individual* mind; secondly, the disease appears to be powerfully *symbolic*; thirdly, the child has no cognitive *knowing* of the meaning even though it is carrying a highly meaning-*full* disease; fourthly, the *system* appears to be able to off-load the distress onto another member of the system, and though we are used to that in other aspects of life it is not usually contemplated where physical diseases are concerned. Surely these things must cause us to think again about our assumptions.

The work of Alfred North Whitehead, David Chalmers, and David Ray Griffin gives us some assistance with the matter of the relationship between matter and 'experience.' They have argued for giving experience the status of a 'fundamental,' but unfortunately none of these philosophers have had meaning-*full* disease in their minds as they have written. In fact they all argue their position from

what is known as 'the mind/body problem,' which we have mentioned previously but must raise again in this context of 'experience.'

The mind/body problem has been at the centre of discussions in
the philosophy of the mind for the last century. It is about how, ultimately, the 'dead matter' of the brain can give rise to the qualities
we call experience or consciousness. It is about how subjective
states we regard as experience can emerge out of what are assumed
to be non-experiencing entities like the body and, particularly, the
brain. If we follow the dualistic models and place subjective experience in the mind, which is seen as separated off from and in tan-
dem with an ultimately 'dead matter' body, we are immediately
faced with one of the major problems of such dualism. How can the
body and the mind, "two totally different types of things ... causal-
ly influence each other" (Griffin 1998, p. 49) Think about the traumatic memories of Margaret's rape, which, in the dualistic models
at least, we suppose are 'mind' things. Many years later, how do
these 'mind' things get transmuted into bleeding in three different
organs, symbolically very closely related to the original trauma?
We also have a very complex example of this problem in Kelly's
story, because it actually involves the minds and bodies of two different people. How can we conceive of her mother's feelings of
abuse being transmuted into the form of her daughter's genital
inflammation?

In my view, an answer begins with the assumption that mind
and body are not distinctly different things. In Margaret's case, the
original experience of the rape is still active in her subject-body, and,
as we address it in therapy, it bursts out in several different bodily
forms. In Kelly's case, mother's experience of sexual abuse is still
active in her subject-body, and in some way Kelly 'experiences' it in
hers, and it bursts out in genital inflammation. If mind and body are
not really different things but the person is a living, experiencing,
embodied whole, living in a rich wider context of mutually interac-
tive other 'wholes' who are constantly helping create or construct
who we are, then we might expect these things rather than be surprised by them. But there are many more things we need to address
before we have more than the germ of an answer.

Let's return to the issue of 'experience.' Chalmers argues that the
'hard' problem of consciousness is really this: Why, when we process
information, do we have any experience at all? For example, we

assume that a machine that can pick up the presence of red light does not have the same awareness or sense of redness that we experience when we see red light. He says:

***

The really hard problem of consciousness is the problem of experience. When we think and perceive, there is a whir of information-processing, but there is also a subjective aspect ... there is something it is like to be a conscious organism. This subjective aspect is experience. When we see, for example, we experience visual sensations: the felt quality of redness, the experience of dark and light ... Then there are bodily sensations, from pains to orgasms; mental images that are conjured up internally; the felt quality of emotion, and the experience of a stream of conscious thought. What unites all these states is that there is something it is like to be in them. All of them are states of experience ... It is widely agreed that experience arises from a physical basis, but we have no good explanation of why and how it arises ... Why doesn't all this information-processing go on "in the dark" free of any inner feel? [Chalmers 1995].

***

Chalmers gives a compelling critique of other philosophers' attempts to explain consciousness, and ends up by claiming that 'to account for conscious experience we need an *extra ingredient* in the explanation' (ibid, p. 7). He assesses various candidates for this extra ingredient, such as non-algorithmic processing, nonlinear and chaotic dynamics, and quantum mechanics, and argues that 'the question of why these processes should give rise to experience is entirely unanswered' (ibid, p. 8).

The problem arises because, in recent history, the way we have viewed the fundamental nature of the world excludes experience. 'Dead matter' (this is not Chalmers' term) does not entail experience. Chalmers' answer is that we should change all that, and see 'experience itself as a fundamental feature of the world, alongside mass, charge, and space-time' (ibid, p. 10). He goes on to organise this idea around the concept of information, and the hypothesis 'that information (at least some information) has two basic aspects, a physical aspect and a phenomenal aspect'(ibid, p. 16). By 'phenomenal aspect' he means an experiential aspect.

Readers can see why this line of thought attracts me. Clinically, I have a host of patients with meaning-*full* diseases. In all of them we see vivid phenomenal experience expressed and structured in the form of meanings, thought, and language. And in all of them we have the informational structures of physical disturbance that, in the case of somatic metaphors, very neatly correspond to the experiences and meanings we have picked up in the phenomenal structures of language. An application of Chalmers' perspective allows me to say that the diseases show both a physical aspect and a phenomenal or experiential aspect.

One of the earliest and simplest examples of meaning-*full* disease that I observed was a woman with a five year history of facial rash, who kept on saying she was keeping a 'brave face' on her husband's depression. There we have it—an experience expressed in the linguistic structure of 'brave face,' and in the physical structure of the facial rash. Since observing this first 'face' story I have seen many others that are similar; here is another:

***

John age 19 presents with frequent very severe outbreaks of a severe itchy, swollen, reddened face that prevents him from working until it settles, and which has required frequent courses of the powerful steroid drug, prednisone. He has a dry skin, a history of some eczema as a child, and various members of his family have eczema. We can probably conclude that he was always at risk of breaking out in eczema. But why now? He does not have any allergies that I can discover. There is a 'story.' He was a rather shy lad. He is an A-grade student who works hard. As he goes through high school he is victimised by school peers, who particularly focus on his appearance. He becomes more self-conscious, and his grades begin to suffer. Eventually at seventeen he pulls out of school and starts a course that requires work-placements in the public eye. The first attack of facial rash occurs on this work placement. We are able to track most subsequent attacks as occurring in relation to stresses *that have to do with public exposure* and attacks on his self-confidence. He and his mother repeatedly use the language of *'facing the public,'* or not being able to *'face'* work.

***

The face is the only part of the body that a 'shy' person cannot hide. Our language is full of the symbolism of the face. We 'face up to people' and we 'look them in the eye.' The face (and its organs: Eyes, mouth, nose) is an embodied vehicle of our self-confidence, our willingness to engage with the 'other' and the world, our readiness to confront. An infant faced with an over-intrusive adult will turn its face away. A child faced with the angry gaze of a parent will crumple and hide its face. The face and the experience of confronting the 'other' are profoundly linked from the earliest times of our lives. With John we have this seamless presentation of the *experience* of facing up to people, the bodily *anatomy* of presenting one's face to people, and the *social crisis* in his work of facing up to people which leads to disturbance in both his felt experience and his anatomy. Here we have the *experiencing body* in powerful relationship with the world. The emphases of the notions of *embodiment* and the *lived body* are well illustrated here. And if Chalmers is right then this is what we would expect. The 'information' of John's shyness has both a physical aspect and a phenomenal or experiential aspect. They are both there, and we should expect them rather than be surprised by them.

Nevertheless, I find Chalmers' concept of 'information' rather sterile as a central organizing concept for experience, probably because, in the past, information has for me been mostly a term for experience-free facts. *Information* is a natural choice of metaphor for a materialistic, data-heavy, computer-centred world. Certainly the world can be conceptualised into structures of information states, information exchange, information spaces, information change, and information as an organizational property. But I am cautious about all reductionisms, and any reduction of the world to 'information' does not fill me with enthusiasm. I suppose it could transform into a less empty term, and a very useful organizing concept, once we assume 'experience' to be fundamental, so that we no longer think of information as merely sterile facts that implicitly deny the experiential richness of life.

Now let's turn to the contributions of Alfred North Whitehead (1861–1947) and David Ray Griffin. Griffin's book, *Unsnarling the World-Knot. Consciousness, Freedom, and the Mind-Body problem* (1998), comprises a very detailed and systematic elaboration and extension of Whitehead's ideas. Whitehead and Griffin, like Chalmers, postulate that experience is a fundamental aspect, potential, or capacity of nature. Griffin's work is of interest because of his emphasis upon the capacity of the physical body, in general, to 'experience.' For him it is not just a matter of the brain being able to 'experience.' If it is true that the body in general can 'experience' then this may be very relevant to the phenomenon of somatic metaphors, and the topic of meaning-*full* disease.

But, before we take this further, we must mention one of the central influences upon many thinkers in the mind/body arena, including Griffin and Whitehead. This influence is the twentieth century awareness that the physical world can no longer be seen as just static spatial matter, but, in Griffin's words, is made up of "an organized system of vibratory streaming of energy" (Griffin 1998, p. 49). In fact, following the theoretical physicist David Bohm (see Broom 1997) we could regard our bodies, and all physical forms, as *semi-stable, structured patterning of energy forms*. If we add Chalmers' notions to the mix, we then have a semi-stable patterning of *energy-filled* forms in which there is both physical structure *and* experience (or experience structure). As a consequence we are very close to the idea that these semi-stable patterned forms carry not only physical structure and experience, but also meanings.

We have referred to these patterned energy forms and structures as organized systems that are *semi-stable*. Death leads to a collapse of these semi-stable patterned energy-filled forms, or at least those we regard as 'living.' The problem with this way of constructing things is that it gives the impression of 'energy' being the fundamental reality, which of course could be the case, but I suspect this is yet another reductionism, which tends to squeeze out other important categories such as consciousness and spirit, or conflates those categories with energy. For that reason I have used the term 'energy-filled' rather than 'energy-based.' I do want to emphasise the energy aspect as a contrast to a 'dead matter' or 'static spatial matter' aspect, but I do not want to posit energy as the end of the story.

Bouratinos (2001) puts it very well:

***

Together, 20th century physics and technology have revealed a reality which can no longer be construed in terms of rationalist fragmentation and vision-mediated physicalism. Zero-point energies, field forces, non-local and non-temporal connections, resonances and non-linear interactions, instabilities, fuzziness, self-organising dynamics, probability patterns and cognitive uncertainties have now become the dominant features of reality. This shows that matter and mind or energy and pattern, which were once conceived to be separate, are now conceived to be one. They are seen as aspects of one another arising out of the same chaotic self-organising process. As this gradually congeals into a specific direction, a division occurs along two fundamental levels of organisation. This division is not intrinsic to the chaotic process itself. It arises from the perceptual and mental sensibilities of man. Below a certain line, things are not measurable. They are endowed with too little energy to become manifest to human perception. They are however computable (at least up to a certain point) on the basis of mathematical extrapolation and model consistency. Above the line, the process does become measurable because it is endowed with sufficient energy to emerge into manifestation. This explains why such fundamental aspects of reality as 'matter' and 'mind,' or 'computability' and 'sensibility,' are now seen by many as just two outstanding points on the same unbroken continuum.

***

Thus we push towards a view of diseases as dysfunctional patterns that have both 'experience' and physical dimensions. Returning to the case of Margaret we might therefore think of her, or any one of us, as a richly structured person based ultimately in patterned energy forms. The form entails patterned systematised physicality, her body, which of course includes the uterus, urinary tract, and breasts. The forms also entail, in her case, a patterned, intensely experiential, and traumatic 'story' very much involving these organs. We could imagine the 'experience' of rape entering and being structured into the totality that is her, her personhood, that cluster of patterned and structured energy forms that is her. The rape is a violation of her personhood, and therefore essentially harmful. It brings a new set of information, distortions of the good, and powerfully re-sets the conformation of the pattern or structure.

Under normal conditions our personhood (the total patterned living whole) appears to be constructed for individual separateness, negotiated intimacy, and loving union. There are variations on this in different cultures, but, in general, the elements seem to be universal. Personhood is not built for violent intrusion or betrayal of trust. These are harmful to the energy-based patterned structures, both physically and subjectively, and they become a negative element in the patterning. Her 'story' and her physicality are thereafter negatively skewed, even determined by these new elements in the patterning. The 'shape' and vitality of her patterned structures are affected and undermined by the rape episode, and eventually they cannot be sustained. There is a collapse, and with the collapse comes illness and disease. In Margaret's case the trigger for this appears to be the minister's betrayal of her trust. She gets depressed. Eventually the rape 'experience' reappears in both physical (bleeding) and subjective (powerful feelings) forms, and for health to be reinstated in her patterned structures the damage has to be repaired in some way.

The energy-based, semi-stable, patterned (schematized; remember chapter eleven) forms, which we recognise as our bodies and our minds, have a certain amount of inherent structure that is perceived, in the case of our bodies by our *sensory organs*, and in the case of our minds by *introspection*. We decide the 'shape' of these structures by perceiving them with the types of capacities we have available to recognize them. The type of body we believe we have is therefore to some extent a 'construction' of our types of sensory apparatus. As Bouratinos says 'it arises from the perceptual and mental sensibilities of man.' We only perceive the forms that we have the capacity to become aware of, because of the unique capacities and limitations of our sensory apparatus which gives us a certain type of and range of vision, hearing, smell and taste, and touch, pain, and position sense. While our range of experiencing of the inherent structure of the world is limited, because of the types of sensory apparatus that we have, we do not doubt that we are picking up on the stable and semi-stable structures of the world in a fairly accurate way. In fact the world picked up in this way is fairly consistent and forms the basis for our trust of measurement and technology.

But our 'seeing' of the patterned forms is not only determined by these fairly reliable but somewhat limited senses. Cultural influences play a huge part in what we see and do not see, what we allow to be visible and what we make invisible. I have already addressed the fact that most clinicians never see 'story' or meaning in a patient's illness. Most societies develop a communal consensus around what forms actually exist and what do not. Again this is partly to do with our sharing of basic sensory abilities, and partly to do with accepting cultural influences as our world-view. Of course people in sub-groups within societies claim to see and experience very different things. For instance, I am doing that when I claim to see meaning in many diseases. In grappling with the notion of experience we do have to confront this issue of what are we seeing and not seeing and what is really real? Which of the things that we see are really stable existing realities that will endure from generation to generation, from culture to culture? Which things are really transient and fundamentally ephemeral cultural constructions?

To emphasize this point I can give an example that raises issues both at the level of our 'reliable' sensory capacities (such as vision) and at the level of cultural belief systems. Recently a very sensible and somewhat conservative medical colleague asked me if I believed in 'aura.' He had had an unusual experience of seeing a red aura around the pelvic area of a sexually abused patient who was very angry, but who had also developed erotic feelings towards him. My colleague was willing to consider any hypothesis, but was inclined to the simple view that the aura represented her anger. Personally speaking, I have never seen an aura, nor have I examined the evidence for such phenomena, and I suppose I can say I neither believe nor disbelieve in such phenomena. But, if I come to his story with a 'dead matter' world-view, I am *very likely* to disparage the idea. In that world-view aura just do not happen. In addition, if both my sensory apparatus (most of us do not see aura as part of our normal physiological range of visual experience) *and* my cultural conditioning are basically oriented to not seeing such phenomena then I am very unlikely to see them or to believe in them. On the other hand, if I believe, as I do, that the notion of patterned energy-based forms and structures is a better framework for conceiving persons than a mere 'dead matter' framework then it is not a big leap for me to imagine that some people may develop a capacity to see elements of our personhood, such as an energy-based aura, that exist just beyond the purview of our normal average perception.

It is not that I really do or do not believe in aura, nor that I particularly want to argue for the existence of aura. The point is that we appear to be dynamic, energy-based, semi-stable, patterned structures that have an inherent physical and experiential aspect. We are constantly experiencing through our sensory structures, and, beyond that, we sometimes find ourselves experiencing in ways that do not seem to be within the normal range of these sensory structures. This is because there are many factors that influence what we do and do not experience. Our construction of the 'shape' of our reality is profoundly influenced by both the limitations of our sensory structures and our cultural beliefs.

Having then set the stage by emphasizing that all the forms of reality that we perceive around us are dynamic, energy-based, patterned structures with seen and unseen dimensions, we can now examine further the possibility, as Griffin and Chalmers would put it, that reality has a *double aspect*. This double aspect is seen in the closeness of matter and experience. This interests me because it is also seen in meaning-*full* diseases, in the startling ways in which the physical manifestations of these diseases mirror the meaning-*full* 'stories.' Patients present in my office with diseases that have a double aspect. It is easy enough to focus down on the single aspect of the physical, but the other aspect is indeed present whether we see it or not.

As already noted, Griffin emphasizes that we have an 'outside' which is our material or physical aspect, our bodies and their parts, and an 'inside' which is our subjective, experiential, conscious aspect. The terms 'outside' and 'inside' do indeed have limitations, but we will stay with them for a moment. The physical aspect is what others see. 'Experience,' which is on the 'inside,' is not what we are for others, but what we are *for ourselves.*' Others cannot know our 'inside' experience directly, though we reveal it most explicitly by our language. They can see 'inside' effects if they are projected on to the 'outside.'

For example, I might have a conflict with someone who gets very angry. I can know that this is so if he *looks* angry, or if he *sounds* angry, both of which are mediated through his body, his 'outside.' He might indeed be angry on the 'inside' and not display this on the outside though if I look hard enough I would usually see something. I could *guess* he might be angry because I know what it feels *like* on the 'inside' in such circumstances. That is empathy. These 'inside' and 'outside' terms are of course just metaphors for the fact that we have this double aspect, that we are organized and constructed for both physicality (the 'outside'-what we are for others) and experience (the 'inside'-what we are for ourselves). Whitehead, Griffin, and Chalmers are saying that experience is fully natural, it is part of 'nature.' By this they mean that experience, or the potential for it is there at the bottom of things, which, if true, means we must see 'matter' differently. It also means we must see bodies very differently. No longer can we tolerate a view of our bodies as based in 'dead matter.' The bodies of my patients with meaning-*full* physical diseases carry meaningful, subjective, and experiential elements. These diseases appear to have an 'outside' which we see in the physical manifestations of the disease. These same diseases also have an 'inside' and that raises an interesting point. Because people talk, and I listen very carefully to their talk, and I have my own 'inside' experience to help me understand, I can pick up the patient's 'inside' meaning. But if they don't talk, or I don't listen, or if I am poorly in tune with my own 'inside' experiences I will not pick it up at all. But whether I listen or not, understand or not, the 'inside' experience/meaning is still present in some form.

The alternative view that nature actually has no 'inside' is a relatively new one. Descartes (1596–1650) may be seen as a major founder of the 'modern age,' or what has become known more recently as *modernity*. He separated the body off into the relatively inert category of matter, which he called *res extensa*, or extended substance. On the other hand, conscious experience became *res cogitans*, or thinking substance. In Descartes' thinking, and during early modernity, the thinking substance became the container for spirituality. The mind/body problem can be seen as rooted in the view that "the fundamental units of nature are material or physical in the sense of being devoid of all experience" (Griffin 1998, p. 83). Thinking substance was carved off from the body. The body was emptied of both 'experience' and spirituality. Spirituality was separated from the body into the thinking substance. Early on the thinking substance had a supernatural and spiritual aspect. But, later again, spirituality became carved off from the thinking substance. Thus, the "dualistic supernaturalism of early modernity" was followed by "the naturalistic materialism of late modernity," which "simply eliminated God and the nonphysical soul" leaving "nature as insentient matter" (ibid, p. 77) alongside some kind of separated mind with no spiritual aspects at all.

Griffin's answer, in respect of experience at least, is to attribute "experience and spontaneity—to all units of nature" (ibid, p. 78). We might baulk at that, if we imagine he is saying that all elements of nature are *conscious*. He is very clear about that not being the case, though others have indeed gone that far. He attributes the potential for experience to all of nature, but sees consciousness as a very advanced aspect of experience found high in the evolutionary tree.

Inch by inch we are arguing for a view of persons and patients with disease, that allows matter and experience, physical disease and 'story' or meaning, to sit as 'one.' The question arises as to how we can talk of human beings in ways that represent this adequately. If the language of mind-plus-body-plus-spirit leads to carving up the person in a way that, in the end, has been powerfully damaging in terms of what we offer our patients then we need other language.

I have argued elsewhere (Broom 2002) that we should talk about patients as 'persons.' The 'person' is not really a combination of mind *plus* body *plus* spirit *plus* soul. We do talk about these aspects of the person in a manner that may suggest that this is so; hence we say "I *have* a body, a mind, a spirit, a soul, and consciousness." But this is a way of talking about different aspects of ourselves. It should not be read as implying that these *are* very separate entities. Anyway, who is this entity that *has* a body? That entity *is* a body. I prefer the alternative language of "I *am* physical, subjective, spiritual, soul-ish, conscious, and relational," which I spelt out in detail in chapter four. I, the whole person, am all of these at one and the same time, in the one and the same space. The dynamic, energy-based, patterned structuring that we have referred to above allows this. I am *being* all these dimensions.

Choosing the right language is difficult. We have to use much description to encompass the complex, multidimensional, *holistic, double-aspect* nature of matter and experience. We need terms that do not divide the person, but it may well be that language will not allow this. The very word *term* suggests we are indulging in the process of categorization, and we have seen that that is always a dividing activity.

But Griffin (following Whitehead) makes an attempt, and conceptualizes events, combining matter and experience, as "actual occasions" (Griffin 1998, p. 127). This is curious language, but on reflection it does seem to work. For example, at this moment I am sitting at my computer. *This* moment is an 'actual occasion,' which includes sitting with my body in a certain posture, my hands and fingers highly coordinated with my brain, with some tightness of the neck and lumbar back muscles, with intense mental focus, and enjoyment of the challenge of getting as clear as possible something that has long been a conviction, something that has helped many patients greatly, and something that may make a contribution to progress in healthcare. All of these elements, and more, make up this 'actual occasion.' There are physical, mental, existential, relational, and spiritual elements hidden within or implicit to this 'actual occasion.' At any clinical consultation both parties (clinician and patient/clients) bring to the event an amazing condensation of such elements. I suppose one could say that each is present as an 'actual occasion,' and from there, out of the special way in which the two interact, another 'actual occasion' emerges. Every clinical story in this book is an example of what emerges when two people with openness and intent allow the physical and the subjective to be present in the same time/space.

Different 'languages' for holism have different limitations. My preferred concepts of 'I am-ness,' or 'personhood' may be suitable for the holistic experience of human beings, but far less suitable for lower forms of life. But, whatever language we choose to capture 'it,' the living organism is a dynamic, communicating, individualized "process of becoming" (Sherbourne 1999, p. 972) based in a double-aspect, matter/experience world, instead of being "an enduring, substantial entity" (ibid) with separated compartments, based in a 'dead matter' world. Experiential events that involve all of our being or personhood are 'actual occasions' with many dimensions. 'Matter' is a very important part of the 'actual occasion,' because matter is an aspect of everything, but it is no longer the rock-bottom reality that skews our thinking to the point that the world is ultimately meaningless, and to the point that our patients' diseases cannot be meaning-*full*.

The language of 'actual occasion,' or 'I am-ness,' or 'personhood,' points to the undivided nature of our being. The language of "I *have* a body, I *have* a mind, etc." is a reflection of our tendency to divide things, essentially a function of the processes of thought and language, and the way we 'construct' the world.

An important aspect of understanding the mind/body problem, which is a result of this dividing of the world, is, as Griffin
(1998, p. 99–100) points out, the fact that we have *two* major forms of
perception. The first is perception through our ordinary five senses (vision, touch, smell, taste, hearing), which give us perception of
the 'outer' world, including observation of our own bodies. This
type of perception also tells us we have a brain structure, but does
not tell us anything about what that brain might 'experience.' We
can examine the brains of animals using these senses but it is
extremely difficult to be sure about what they *experience*. Our
knowledge of our own experience comes from the second form of
perception, *introspection*, which allows us perception of our inner
experience. But, in turn, introspection can tell us nothing about the
structure of the brain.

McGinn (1991), another philosopher of the mind, asserts that we
are stuck with mind/body separation because we are constructed to
perceive them in a separated way. Basically he is saying that the two
types of perception automatically divide matter and experience; that
is how we construct things. His bleak conclusion is that therefore the
mind/body problem is insoluble.

We might temper that extreme position, and argue that ordinary
human experience is indeed constrained or structured by these two
modes of perception, but not necessarily shut down inside the limits of these two modes. Moreover, as Griffin points out, the strong
sense of separateness that we have of mind and body, which
McGinn attributes entirely to these two modes of perception, may
actually be due more to the powerful influence of the Cartesian tradition than truly reflect the limits of our perception. That is, we
could see the separation of mind and body as in part a "cultural
exaggeration" (Griffin 1998, p. 102) rather than just a perceptual
inevitability. After all, prior to modernity, and in many contemporary non-Western cultures, physical reality was/is not so divided off
from subjective and spiritual reality. This contradicts the idea that
the division is an inevitable consequence of the use of our normal
perceptual modes.

We can conclude that the two modes of perception are looking at
the same reality (which truly has the two aspects) in different *ways*.
Perception does divide. Categorization divides. Water is divided
into 'cold' and 'wet' but we still comprehend water as a 'whole.' Our

living experience can be divided into 'experience' and the 'physical' by these two modes of perception but we can still see the 'whole.' We should not conclude that reality is *ultimately* divided on the basis of the separating effects of selective perception. How we *handle* reality should be distinguished from reality itself. In that context I really like Griffin's comment that "it is arguably the mind's identification of itself with its *conscious* experience that creates the illusion of the mind's isolation from the world" (Griffin 1998, p. 107) The lesson is that we should be careful to avoid jumping to conclusions as to what mind really is.

If matter and experience are one then it may follow that not just the brain but the whole body is capable of 'experience' at some level, because the body is not merely 'dead matter' organized in a way to give an appearance of life. Even the fingers and the toes have this double aspect of materiality and experience. We have been taught that experience is really confined to the mind/brain combination. We could summarize the recent history of mind/body concepts by saying that the capacity for experience has been carved off from the body to be situated in the mind/brain, which is in a sense in a separate compartment sitting above the shoulders. And, from there, sophisticated meanings or 'story' have been carved off into the separated mind (giving rise to the mind/body problem).

But, in reality, the central nervous system and the peripheral nerves are specialized extensions of one another. Do we really think fundamental experience *starts* in the nervous tissue only as the impulses reach neck level and above? To be sure, *aspects* of that experience are dependent on those high level brain structures. A pain experience, for example, begins at the finger, and may be altered, managed, controlled at the level of the brain, but I think the experience *begins* at the site of stimulus. The brain may be more an organizer and developer of experience, a generator of more sophisticated experience.

Whitehead and Griffin argue that low level organisms, which are without sophisticated central nervous systems, but which do react to various stimuli, are actually 'experiencing' in a primitive way. But scientific materialism "presupposes the ultimate fact of an irreducible brute matter" (Whitehead, in Griffin 1998, p. 117), which implies these low level organisms, and the painful finger, are not 'experiencing' and do not have any form of subjectivity.

We also need to avoid making the mistake of thinking that 'experience' is the same as consciousness and thought. Griffin (1998) argues that we experience ourselves as an organic unity; and this unity appears to us to be akin to other elements of the world, albeit having a more sophisticated form. There is an inner aspect, an 'inside viewpoint,' to this experience, and for us this involves consciousness and sophisticated self-consciousness.

Our continuity with the rest of nature suggests there is a continuity of this 'inside' viewpoint across the many species, though as we go down the evolutionary tree it will have less sophistication and less self-reflective elements. The more sophisticated forms such as consciousness, which we recognize in ourselves, are derivative elements of the capacity for experience. They are not actually essential to all experience though they are essential to *our human experience.* Whitehead, in *Modes of Thought* (1938, p. 116), calls the more sophisticated forms of experience 'vivid accidents.' They are characteristic of our experience but not crucial to all experience, wherever it is found in non-human realities. In this view unborn babies, infants, and the sleeping adult are indeed 'actual occasions' involving experiencing, but where cognition or *thinking about the experience* is not a *main* manifestation of the experience. Thus, while an experience may be extremely vivid, it need not involve adult human types of thinking or self-reflection. The experience is a unity of 'reception, enjoyment, and action—(it) is not dependent on conscious operations' (Griffin 1998, p. 126).

Consciousness is seen as a sophisticated *derivative* of the capacity for experience. Experience is the sum total of the unitary and unified elements of 'actual occasions(s)' that have inherent bodily, subjective, temporal, and spatial aspects. 'There can be no "bare" grasping of an object, devoid of subjective feeling' (Griffin 1998, p. 128). The very phrase 'physical experience,' which we can all relate to, captures the reality we are talking about. I was fascinated recently by a report in our local newspaper featuring a study that purported to prove that fish caught on a hook actually experienced pain! Why would we imagine that they did not, apart, of course, from avoiding guilt at inflicting suffering? The pain of the fish might be different to the pain we experience. But it is easy to see that, if we tend to identify experience (and suffering) with higher forms of *consciousness,* it would be tempting to begin to deny vivid experience (including pain) to lower forms of life with more primitive forms of consciousness.

If we are going to attribute experience to just about everything then we need to allow for different levels of experience. This is a hugely complex topic. Griffin (again following and developing Whitehead's views) says the first stage of an experience involves *physical prehensions*—a taking account of *other* actualities (say a red object). The second phase is *conceptual* where we develop a mental object of that which is prehended in the first phase. This leads to the *feeling or experience of redness*. This is mentality—and it's about *appetition*. It is about being drawn towards or away from the red ball. In this second phase, using the example of the red object, *redness* is the conceptual feeling of that which I have prehended or taken account of. In the third phase there are *propositions* that are combinations of the first two. So we can say *this ball is red*. The object in this phase is not the ball but the proposition itself. The proposition is very interesting because it can be manipulated. Propositions are very creative. They can lure feelings, indeed their main role is as a "lure for feelings.' The fourth phase involves the emergence of *intellectual feelings*, where conscious judgments about this scenario emerge. 'There is integration of a propositional feeling (from the third phase) with primitive physical feelings (from the first phase)' (Griffin 1998, p. 130).

The fourth phase intellectual feelings involve consciousness, including conscious perceptions, and cognition or judgments. It also involves *negation*, a capacity generally regarded as the 'triumph of consciousness.' Achieving the level of *the ball is red* is a very primitive act of consciousness. We see that in infants when they exclaim 'red ball!' We know that they have developed much further when they burst into tears at being given a green ball instead of the red. *The ball is not red* is the triumph of consciousness. "More precisely, consciousness involves the contrast between what is and what might be, between fact and theory' (Griffin 1998, p. 131). Interestingly, though, while we give great credence to our most sophisticated consciousness 'in most occasions of experience, the fourth phase does not occur, or is latent at best' (Griffin 1998, p. 131). We operate on a vast raft of first, second, and third phase experiences.

I have emphasized that there are, indeed, ways of thinking about persons, the world, and nature that allow us to conceive of meaning-*full* disease as soundly grounded, in a world that has the double-aspect of matter and experience. The arguments of Chalmers, Griffin, and Whitehead propose experience as a crucial fundamental in reality. They unite experience and matter in a way that is helpful in getting past the unfortunate separation of mind and body. They also help us understand gradations in the capacity to experience. Animals, human fetuses and infants, and older humans, all do 'experience' in some way, and their experiences all have both subjective and physical aspects. I am not sure that experience is at rock-bottom, but I think it is much closer to rock-bottom than we have allowed ourselves to imagine, and because this is so we can begin to feel much more comfortable about the close linkage of physical disease and 'meanings.'

CHAPTER THIRTEEN

Meaning-*full* disease and spirit

For millennia, the peoples of the world have honoured the role of spirit in life, but during the last few hundred years Western culture has increasingly operated out of a physico-materialist world-view. It is interesting then to see that some philosophers are edging towards what some have called the 're-enchantment' of nature, by emphasizing a fundamental role for 'experience.' There are, of course, many people taking much more daring steps than this, towards rediscovering the role of spirit in life.

I recall starting training in psychiatry in 1981, and feeling the pervasive professional restraints, at least in New Zealand, upon any discussion of spirit or spiritual values, and, indeed, the lingering and very prevalent twentieth-century hostility amongst mental health professionals towards religion. By the early 1990s, it was increasingly acceptable amongst New Zealanders of European origin to talk (albeit cautiously) about spirit, especially if it concerned the spirituality of our indigenous people, the Maori. It seemed that, for a while at least, it was 'safe' to own the existence of spirituality 'over there,' to not let it get too close. Now, in 2005, the term spirituality is used widely, and with increasing ease in many forums, though it actually means very different things to different people.

In the face of this, and because of my own predilections, it would be wrong to limit any discussion of spirit and meaning-*full* disease to philosophers' postulations of a new, or renewed, intimacy between experience and material aspects of the universe. In addition, I am not ready, as some are, to reduce whatever people may mean by spirit to categories and dimensions of reality such as energy, information, or experience, even though I have found such categories useful in elucidating aspects of meaning-*full* disease. Finally, our focus has been upon 'meaning.' Few people would argue against the idea that issues and concepts of meaning have been at the centre of all traditions of spirituality. Only a dyed-in-the-wool radical materialist could focus on dimensions of meaning and yet refuse to consider those of spirituality.

How then to approach meaning-*full* disease with spirit definitely in focus? It is difficult for me to honour the role of spirit without being tempted into a grandiose fantasy that I might somehow write a chapter that truly captures the essence of the relationship of spirit to matter, and therefore to meaning-*full* disease. That temptation has passed. But on the other hand a desire remains to do justice to this crucial topic. My way of resolving the dilemma, for this volume at least, is to stay true to my determination to proceed from clinical cases, from phenomena, from my grounding substrate, towards general principle, rather than the other way round. We will therefore consider several examples of disease and body dysfunction which appear to me to highlight the possible role of spirit in relation to meaning-*full* disease.

A few preliminary scene-setting remarks are needed. When I use the words *spirit* or *spiritual*, I refer to the sense many of us have of a dimension, or of dimensions, beyond the narrow visibility of ordinary physical existence. Wilber (in *The Marriage of Sense and Soul: Integrating Science and Religion*) provides a masterful review of the Great Chain of Being, which is the time-hallowed and pervasively cross-cultural belief that

***

"reality is a rich tapestry of interwoven levels, *reaching from matter to body to mind to soul to spirit*" [Wilber 1998, italics original].

***

Wilber deviates from the metaphor of *chain*, preferring the idea that these dimensions sit together as a *nest* rather than a *chain*, with each 'senior' dimension enfolding the others, spirit being the most senior dimension.

The notion of spirit is a difficult one in the modern world because, while many people are seeking a spiritual dimension, there is great variety in such seeking. Some people have a rather limited concept of spirit, which may in some respects be compatible with a materialistic view of the universe. Spirit as 'beauty' or other ideals might be an example of this. Spirit is in this case reduced to human values. Others are inclined to conflate spirit with, or reduce spirit to, notions of 'consciousness' as a transcendent dimension. Thus, in some circles, spirituality rests upon a transpersonal consciousness, and meditative practice, but can be essentially atheistic. Others, of course, retain a belief in a supra-human being, God, who may be either an immanent presence, or, alternatively, a transcendent 'other,' or indeed both. And, of course, there are traditions that mix these emphases in a variety of ways. But, despite this diversity, there are some generic elements of spirituality germane to this discussion of meaning-*full* disease.

I recall an annual conference of the New Zealand Association of Psychotherapists in the early 1990s, when the topic of the conference was *The Place of Soul in Psychotherapy*. The conference did not stop to ponder any distinction between the categories of soul and spirit and it was my impression that the title embraced both. Anyway, this was a novel and, at the time, daring focus for the Association, and, indeed, some members stayed away in protest. I attended one workshop in which the forty people attending had real difficulty establishing a starting-place for discussion, partly because of the wide diversity of participants, which included Buddhists, Christians, atheists, and agnostics. Finally, in frustration, we divided into groups of three to discuss and define what we actually meant by 'soul.' I was struck by the extraordinary concordance that emerged. Virtually all groups returned saying that in using the word 'soul' they were emphasizing that it captured something *within*, something that was deeper, wider, and broader than those experiences captured and defined using words like mind, body, feeling, emotion, thought, and even ideals like beauty. It seemed that all of us had a similar *sense* of soul or spirit.

But, if we try and define spirit further, we do see real differences. For example, Epstein (2004) recently provided a definition of spiritual in an article in the journal Advances in Mind/Body Medicine:

***

"The term *spiritual* means essentially the presence, influence, and priority, of invisibility in our visible world, this latter world we call objective material reality. We become connected to Spirit if we accept the truth of this unknown existence, so much so that we pledge ourselves allegiance with this higher intangible reality and accept its governance in/over our lives, even though it is not apprehendable by our five senses in this material time-space dimensional existence."

***

Epstein emphasizes the 'presence, influence, and priority' of the spiritual in the day-to-day existence of beings. I really like this, given that the phenomena of meaning-*full* disease demand a unitary, holistic perspective. On the other hand I differ from Epstein when he says we *become* connected to Spirit by acknowledging spirit. This is a very compartmentalised and conditional view. I would say we *are* spiritual *whether we like it or not*. Speaking from the perspective of the whole, our being *is* spiritual, *is* subjective, *is* material, *is* relational, *is* conscious, and *is* unconscious. We can certainly neglect, deaden, or foster the life of the spirit (which I suspect is what he really means) just as we can neglect, deaden, or foster our feelings and our physicality.

Another issue he raises is that of the spirit being essentially *invisible*. I am sure there are spiritual realities or dimensions that are mostly invisible. But I resist too much division into the *visible* and the *invisible* when it comes to spirit. Such division can imply that the ordinary world, the visible world, the world of matter and things, is fundamentally empty of spirit. That is the post-Cartesian world, the physico-materialist world of modernist science. In reaction to this perspective there have indeed been trends towards the 're-enchantment' of nature as already mentioned. The presence of spirit in the world, and the idea of spirit underpinning the world, have been long-held assumptions in many traditions, and now, as we have seen, the 'experience' philosophers are edging back towards something similar.

While I accept there are 'invisibles' in our lives I am cautious about constructing them in a way that creates a separate compartment for the spiritual. I believe Wilber is resisting the same thing when he emphasizes the Great Nest rather than the Great Chain of Being. The Chain is a rather linear concept which more easily invites division than does the Nest. Some of that which is invisible is so because we have made it so; we have constructed it that way, often in the way we talk about it.

Having made these points, let's turn to some stories. I have chosen four that have stood out for me as having an extra quality that seems to emphasize the presence of spirit. This might be seen to be contradictory. After all, the *I am spiritual* construction of personhood would suggest that spirit is to be seen in all situations. That is true. But just as the physical aspect, or story aspect, may become very obvious in some cases, so this is true of the spiritual aspect. I freely acknowledge that if I could 'see' better then some things currently invisible to me may become much more obvious than they are now. The four stories I now present are examples where I suddenly became aware of 'something else,' of being pushed beyond my usual awareness. The issue may of course be much more a matter of my awareness than that these cases were 'more spiritual.'

***

The first is that of patient T., who suffered from the precancerous oral condition of leukoplakia, and went on to develop cancer of the mouth. Her story was originally elsewhere (Broom 1997), and the theoretical implications have been discussed in earlier chapters here. I want now to pick up the possible 'spiritual' aspects. In summary, she developed a nasty pre-cancerous condition of the mouth, which later became cancerous and required reconstructive surgery. As the story unfolded, it became clear that the disease related to her shame at causing her father's death (by suicide), and that her father was a dentist. We discovered that the disease developed at the exact age her father committed suicide. During one session she presented a dream, and explorations around that led to some important shifts in regard to her sense of responsibility for his death (see Broom 1997 for detail). But the important point here is her report that after that session, while driving away from our Centre, she experienced an extraordinary 'joy' which she described as being in the centre of her being. And this joy persisted for days, and then weeks. It was like something had happened in her 'core.' She found herself able to talk with confidence in groups and formal meetings, something we had not even talked about in our sessions together. And later we found that her mouth condition had disappeared, after being active for more than two decades.

***

I have always felt that there was a 'numinous' quality to this particular encounter. The way she originally came to me utterly 'ready' to do something, the way the story unfolded almost without effort, the 'spooky' congruence of the extraordinary and symbol-laden life facts with the nasty character of the condition, the ease and rapidity with which the therapy developed, the spontaneous provision of a crucial dream, the extraordinary joy welling up inside her, the pervasive unexpected positive effects in her life, and the rapid receding of the oral condition, have all left me with a sense of wonder and a sense of 'spirit,' of something working with us that was much bigger and more fundamentally lively than my usual quiver of resources. Was this relatively unfettered spirit at work? Sometimes there seems to be an amazing conjunction of forces and goodness of fit, a rightness of timing or synchronicity, an unconstrained energy, an uncanny emergence of the truth linked with creative forward movement, and with all this a loving and generous outcome. It feels like spirit is not only present but actively at work in an unfettered way.

I want now to turn to a very different case.

***

Beth is 49 years old and has a very traumatic history, partly to do with her violent father, and very significantly compounded by the accidental death of her 7 year old sister Catherine, whilst in Beth's care, at age 15. The impact of this tragic event for Beth was hugely compounded by the failure of her parents to perceive the seriousness of her calls for help at the time the tragedy unfolded, their own need to protect themselves from guilt resulting in a tendency to cover up the facts at the inquest, and a tendency to project the blame on to Beth. Beth had suffered a variety of physical problems over the years, each of which were in their own ways fascinating examples of the expression of traumatic meaning-*full* events in bodily form. For brevity's sake I will describe one session with Beth that illustrates some remarkable and immediate relationships between meaning and body.

Beth arrived at a session rather jubilant, having won a prize in a competition. But she was also preoccupied with a curious circumstance. A friend, who could have had no prior knowledge of the competition, had e-mailed her the night before saying that if she replied by e-mail *immediately*, then the next day she would win a prize of some sort. Beth complied, unaware that the next day she would be offered the chance to enter a competition. In our session Beth and I exchanged views on esoteric subjects such as synchronicity, time/space concepts, and influence at a distance, topics that appeared to have relatively little interest for her.

I then remembered the dream she had had decades before, a few days before Catherine's death. In that dream she had been 'warned' that Catherine was about to die. While I was wondering to myself about this, Beth exclaimed that if her friend's e-mail about the competition was *not* a coincidence then her dream providing foreknowledge about Catherine's death was not a coincidence either.

She went on to mention several occasions when as an adult she had other experiences of apparent foreknowledge, and that after one such event she attended a Spiritualist Church to get some answers. At this point in the session she started to get uneasy. She described a church meeting where a man leading the meeting went round the room making perceptive comments about individuals. He arrived at her and said "Your father and you. ..." but she was unable to complete the statement. Apparently she fled the meeting after his comments were made.

But in our session, at the point at which she was telling me what he said, she became agitated, and could not go on. I pressed her to tell me what it was he had said about her and her father, but she said her head had gone blank, she could not remember. Suddenly she gripped her head and exclaimed: "I've got a terrible headache, I cannot go on." Moments later she complained of light-headedness.

We waited for a short while, and then talked about how she was getting to some intense feelings and how unmanageable they were. She said she felt like she was being 'flooded.' We talked about how she closed the doors on her feelings to avoid being flooded, and how they got expressed in this instance in sudden blinding headache and light-headedness.

We agreed that she was more frequently allowing herself come closer to those feelings, but it was dangerous. She then talked about what had happened two days before. She had been doing some work preparation at her table. The television was on, but she was focused on her work and hardly conscious of the programme which turned out to be an Oprah Winfrey programme on Teenagers Angry with their Parents. Suddenly she found herself very agitated, and compelled to ring me to feel safe. She had the strong perception she might be a danger to someone.

I have little doubt that she had lived with an underlying rage towards various adults including her parents who, in her view, had not adequately carried their responsibilities for Catherine's death. I ventured that I could understand such anger given the circumstances, and wondered if the man at the church had said anything about such feelings towards her father. Again she became agitated, and then said she could imagine a picture of a 'court-room with many adults in it, and they were all burning.' That is as far as she could go. She asked me if I thought she might harm someone. I replied that I felt that she had lived a long time with a huge anger towards adults who had failed her, and with a sense of inappropriate responsibility that had never been adequately lifted. I wondered whether one of the ways she was stuck was that underneath she felt her anger was so fierce that it could culminate in violence. Certainly, internalized, it had over the years wreaked havoc with her body, and the headache and light-headedness in the session was a vivid immediate example of the connections between her intense feelings with respect to her father, and expression in the body. I suggested that our task was to go near the anger in a way that allowed it to be experienced and acknowledged without flooding her too much. She agreed and seemed to leave the session with some lightness.

***

This interesting story is pervaded by a sense of the *transpersonal*. There are things happening between people, across distant space, and across time. The material cannot be locked up inside the confines of the individual. There is the 'warning' in Beth's dream about Catherine's death which occurred some days later, the 'prediction' by a friend of Beth winning a prize, the synchronicity in our session of my wonderings about the earlier dream and Beth mentioning it within moments of my wondering, the intuitions and statements of the Spiritualist minister, and the triggering by the Oprah Winfrey show. It is like everything was happening at once to a certain end. From a meaning-*full* disease perspective it is of course fascinating that the unmanageability of it all created an explosion in the body; a blinding headache.

Again, as with Eunice, there is this powerful sense of direction, and 'coincidence,' perhaps governed by invisible but very present forces. In the case of Eunice the direction is unambiguously positive. In Beth's case I am not so sure.

These sorts of events are not confined to my clinic.

***

Many years ago I visited Canon Jim Glennon at the Anglican Cathedral in Sydney, Australia. I had read of the weekly healing services he conducted there, and was interested to explore his approach. The healing service I attended involved a congregation of perhaps three to five hundred people, and, frankly, it seemed a rather ordinary Anglican service. But I was fascinated by the story he proffered as we engaged in a discussion around how he got into the healing ministry.

He had been visiting a parishioner in hospital. She had ovarian cancer, and it was so advanced and extensive that she had what is called a 'frozen pelvis'; that is, the solid tumour filled the pelvis. She asked him to pray for her, which he did, and then left. That night she experienced a sense of burning in the pelvis that went on for hours. The next morning she was taken to the operating theatre for insertion of radium implants, to provide radiotherapy treatment of the tumour. But, first, she was examined, and to the surgeon's astonishment the tumour was gone, and the procedure was abandoned.

***

Spontaneous remissions of cancer are well-documented (O'Regan and Hirshberg 1993), and I have no reason to doubt the veracity of Glennon's story. I have pondered it many times, especially as I have come to realize that 'matter,' as we know it through the five senses, *appears* very structured and stable, but can be equally well described as energy-based and semi-stable. Moreover, the insights of theoretical physicist David Bohm emphasize that reality has both *explicate* and *implicate* dimensions. The explicate dimension is what we perceive with our five senses. It has obvious structure and stability. The implicate dimension is there *inside* the explicate, but is invisible, more 'fluid' and energy-based. I can therefore imagine some force 'stirring' in the implicate dimension that leads to radical change in the explicate dimension. The important point is that while the explicate dimension relies on a level of structure and stability this aspect is *not rigid*. For me, that means miracles can happen, but are not common. Indeed the term 'miracle' may mean what it does because its very nature reflects two important realities: That the world has a semi-stable structure, and that it is not finally rigid, so conditions do arise when the *implicate*, the *spiritual*, the *invisible*, or whatever, can bring about rapid change in the semi-stable explicate world.

These things sometimes come much closer to home.

***

Some years ago I developed an unusual lesion on my left-arm about five centimetres in diameter. From a medical perspective it looked as if the skin had died or, technically speaking, atrophied. The skin over the lesion became so thin and delicate that I could see tiny vessels beneath it, and I had to cover it up to avoid it getting damaged when doing manual work. It neither progressed nor remitted over several years. I had never seen anything quite like it, and did not consult a medical practitioner because I didn't think anyone would know what it was. I accepted it as one of those small mysteries in life. But I do wish now that I had photographed it!

Two or three years after the onset of the lesion, and during a period of my own personal psychotherapy, I had two very vivid dreams concerning my father. When I was a young doctor aged twenty-six, my father died at age fifty-nine of lung cancer. It was a very difficult time for both of us. He found it extremely difficult to acknowledge that he had a fatal disease, and I was drawn into a very painful process of providing (false) reassurance and hope. Though I was left with very positive memories of my relationship with him, there was one thing, over the many years following, that seemed to hover around the edges of my consciousness. I sometimes wondered whether I too might die of cancer in my fifties. There was an intangible sense that I was bound in to him in some way, and it seemed that the way he died, and the age at which he died, could in some way be predictive for me. But I mostly brushed it aside, and certainly gave the matter no systematic thought. It was more a recurring thought than a preoccupation.

Let's return now to the dreams, especially the second. In the dream I walked towards, and then into, a rest home or hospice on a rise overlooking an Arcadian park-like setting. This mansion had an upper story with a balcony, upon which there was a canvas deckchair with wooden framework. I was lying on this chair. The notable thing about the chair was that there were round cancerous secondaries, or metastatic deposits, in the wooden framework, and about the same size as the round lesion on my left arm. It was very clear in the dream that the cancerous deposits were in the wooden framework and not in me (the person lying on the chair).

Following this dream, I pondered the nature of my relationship with my father, and what appeared to be issues of separation/individuation from him, and the sense I had of not grieving his death adequately. The next Sunday morning I decided to visit his grave, and spent time thinking and feeling through some of the old events of our lives together and also his death. After an hour or so I returned home with a quiet sense that I had done what was right for me at that point, but no sense of why it had emerged at that time. It is important to note that the arm lesion itself had *not* been in my conscious awareness during this period of consideration of the dreams.

The next day I noticed that my left arm was itchy, and examination showed that the lesion was reddened. Over the next ten days the 'dead' skin of the lesion completely regenerated and the skin returned to normal. And then I noticed that my background concern that somehow I was tied to my father in respect of cancer and death in the sixth decade had also disappeared. Eight years have elapsed since this event and the feelings have not returned.

On the face of it then, it seems that the same 'story' was being told in my mild conscious concern about possibly dying in my sixth decade, in the coin-shaped lesion in my physical body, and in the dreams concerning coin-shaped cancerous deposits in the deck-chair presumably representing my unconscious functioning. Put another way, I had this awareness in my consciousness of some sort of connectedness, or lack of separation from, or over-identification with my father and his illness. And the same thing was represented in the language of the body for several years in the form of the arm lesion. And then, in the course of psychotherapy, dreams emerged with a different languaging of the same thing.

But what is of interest here is that I had not been actively pursuing or working in psychotherapy on this theme of my relationship with my father. Certainly I had not raised the issue of fear of dying by sixty with the therapist. And the coin-shaped lesion had never seemed very important. Something almost gratuitous seemed to happen. I am now just over sixty years old, and I assume I will never know if this experience had any relevance to getting to this age, though I have wondered.

***

Of course, serendipitous things happen to many people, and in diverse ways. But, in all of the examples given above, there is an element of surprise, of an out-of-the-ordinary breaking through of something else, of 'grace' elements, of a dimension beyond our individual control. We (I, and the patient) were there, and participated, even to the point of permitting them to happen, but not in the stronger sense of *making* them happen. There was an extra reminder within these 'actual occasions' that spirit is alive and well. I believe that the dimension of spirit underpins every living and healing process, but sometimes it manifests in a way that particularly draws my attention.

All of the four examples given above involved the body, and vivid manifestations in the body. At least three of them were mean-ing-*full* diseases (or body dysfunctions). And this leads me to another assertion. If we believe that the organism is spiritual, unitary, and *essentially undivided* (even though somewhat differentiated into schemata) then the scene is set for a *spiritual* description of meaning-*full* disease. Just as holism demands the possibility of a *physical description* of disease and a *subjective storied description*, so it demands a *spiritual description*.

Another way I have of explaining this is in the metaphor of 'cuts' through the data (see Broom 2002). We have a 'whole' that is made up of all kinds of data: Physical, subjective, social, cultural, spiritual, and ecological data or constituents. If we take a physical 'cut' through the combined data we observe only those elements that match our intention to examine the physical. In other words, as an observer I look at the physical elements but not the rest. If I take a meanings or story 'cut' I focus upon those aspects, somewhat neglecting the physical elements. Logically then we should also be able to take a family 'cut,' a cultural 'cut,' and a spiritual 'cut.' A fully integrative perspective of any disease would require the availability of all of these 'cuts.' Therefore, I really do believe that we cannot properly understand meaning-*full* or experience-full disease without an exploration of the relationships between body and spirit. It will not be enough to comprehend the relationship of these disorders to language, infant development, experience, or any other category already discussed in this book.

What would it mean to develop a spiritual view of disease? I do not intend expanding this too far—it has to be the subject of another volume—but I can point to what I think is important.

Firstly, there is the issue of spirit and *relationship*. I would say that relationship is one of the fundamentals of life. Most stories in this book emphasize the emergence of disease relative to experiences we have with important 'others.' I suggest that we will also find that disease frequently emerges when we are spiritually dysfunctional, when we break certain spiritual foundations, when our *relations* with the spiritual dimension, or the 'Other' are problematic. But, clearly it is all very complex. The notions of multidimensional reality and multifactorial causation would suggest that a major 'fault' in our physical 'structure' *plus* a minor 'fault' in our spiritual 'structure' might actually have a greater impact on health than, say, a minor 'fault' in our physical structure *plus* a major 'fault' in our spiritual 'structure.' It will depend on a balance of factors. Every case will be different.

Secondly, much of what I have discussed in this book represents *horizontal* types of data. The capacity of matter for experience, the non-verbal experiences of the foetus and infant, and the compounding subsequent experiences of the child and the adult, are really all *this-life*, ordinary space-time data. If we accept the existence of the spiritual, a depth-*vertical* dimension, we can imagine that the contributions from this dimension to meaning-*full* disease may be rather different. For instance, the emergence of an illness in a culture may be less a function of what actual historical life-experiences the *individual* has had, and more a representation of the spiritual state of that culture. We have seen hints of that in the last chapter in the case of the daughter carrying the 'marks' of the sexual abuse suffered by her mother. A spiritual model of disease could reflect many things beyond the space-time history of the *individual*.

Thirdly, the physical world is clearly sufficiently structured for us to have developed elaborate systematic methods of exploration of it. We can measure it, and predict, at least to some extent, how it will behave. Science has thrived on the semi-stable structure of the physical dimension of the world. But if there is a 'senior' spiritual dimension we should not be surprised when it upsets this stability of the physical dimension, when 'miracles' occur, when suddenly there is a supra-event. There is room in our model for such events, but in the 'dead matter' model of physico-materialism such events must be ruled out. In a spiritual model we can live with the normal 'rules' of the semi-stable reality, but at the same time be open to the serendipitous and gracious expansions characteristic of the spiritual. In a spiritual world we should expect supra-events, but also appreciate the deep spiritual underpinning of ordinary life. This also implies there will be patients and clients that we fail miserably with utilizing approaches and technologies that implicitly take no account of the spiritual, or, for some reason, restrict the opportunities of the spiritual, the implicate, or the invisible.

Fourthly, it makes no sense to have an either/or view of reality. Some authors, like Epstein (cited above), are adamant that psychotherapy and spiritual approaches are inimical to one another. But a unitary view of the person allows very different 'cuts,' and very different approaches to the same reality. It appalls me how often we establish our own approach to our patients as the *only* approach. It is a very different matter to say that the *best* approach in this or that case might indeed be surgery, or couple therapy, or abandonment of materialism along with spiritual exercises, or, perhaps best of all, some combination of all these modes.

Fifthly, and finally, acknowledging the numinous, the presence of spirit in ordinary life, the fountain of life energising all things, creates a very lively framework for being with people. While we are trained and skilled, sometimes very trained and very skilled, we can hold our skills and training lightly. We are spiritual beings able to open ourselves to the moment. We are not essentially alone with our patients. If we open ourselves we find ourselves working in concert with God, but we are not God. We need not burden ourselves with being the ultimate expert, with knowing all that needs to be known. We do have expertise but, in the moment, we must hold this ever so lightly, and abandon ourselves to whatever new things there are that might emerge. That is the spirit in which I discover the most useful outcomes with my patients.

BIBLIOGRAPHY

Advances in Mind/Body Medicine (2001). 17: 3–59.

Baldwin, T. (Ed.) (2004). *Maurice Merleau-Ponty: Basic Writings*. London: Routledge.

Bohm, D., & Peat, D.F. (2000). *Science, Order, and Creativity*. London: Routledge, 2nd ed.

Bouratinos, E. (2001). The reality between: Toward an epistemology for the paranormal. Network. *The Scientific and Medical Network Review*, No. 77, December, pp. 12–17.

Broom, B.C. (1997). *Somatic Illness and the Patient's Other Story. A Practical Integrative Mind/Body Approach to Disease for Doctors and Psychotherapists*. London: Free Association Books.

Broom, B.C. (2000). Medicine and story: a novel clinical panorama arising from a unitary mind/body approach to physical illness. *Advances in Mind/ Body Medicine, 16*: 161–207.

Broom, B.C. (2002). Somatic metaphor: A clinical phenomenon pointing to a new model of disease, personhood, and physical reality. *Advances in Mind/Body Medicine 18*: 16–29.

Bullmore, E., Joyce, H., Marks, I.M., & Connolly, J.J. (1992). A computerised quality assurance system (QAS) on a general psychiatric ward: Towards efficient clinical audit. *Mental Health* 1: 257–263.

Carroll, R. (2005). Neuroscience and the 'law of the self.' In: N.Totton (Ed.), *New Dimensions in Body Psychotherapy* (pp. 13–29). Maidenhead: Open University Press.

Chalmers, D.J. (1995). Facing up to the problem of consciousness. *J. of Consciousness Studies*, 2: 200–219.

Chiozza, L.A. (1998 a). *Hidden Affects in Somatic Disorders. Psychoanalytic Perspectives on Asthma, Psoriasis, Diabetes, Cerebrovascular Disease, and Other Disorders*. Madison: Psychosocial Press.

Chiozza, LA. (1998 b). *Why Do We Fall Ill? The Story Hiding in the Body*. Madison: Psychosocial Press.

de Quincey, C. (2002). Nature has a mind of her own. Network. *The Scientific and Medical Network Review*. No. 80, December, pp.6–9.

Engel, G.L. (1977). The need for a new medical model: A challenge for biomedicine. *Science 196*: 129–136.

Epstein, G. (2004). Mental imagery: The language of the spirit. *Advances in Mind-Body Medicine, 20*: 4–10.

Foss, L. (2002). *The End of Modern Medicine*. Albany, New York: State University of New York Press.

Griffin, D.R. (1998). *Unsnarling the World-Knot. Consciousness, Freedom, and the Mind-Body Problem*. London: University of California Press.

Griffith, J.L., and Griffith, M.E. (1994). *The Body Speaks: Therapeutic Dialogues for Mind-Body Problems*. New York: Basic Books.

Griffin, D. (1998). *Unsnarling the World-Knot*. London: University of California Press.

Grigg, R. (1997). *The Tao of Being. Lao Tzu's Tao Te Ching Adapted for a New Age* (p. xvi). Atlanta: Element Books Limited.

Groddeck, G., (1928). In a paper given before the Psychotherapeutic Congress, Translated by Collins, V.M.E. In: L. Schacht (Ed.) (1977), *The Meaning of Illness. Selected Psychoanalytic Writings by George Groddeck*. London: The Hogarth Press and the Institute of Psychoanalysis, pp. 208–10.

Hay, L.L. (1982). *Heal your Body*. Concord (Australia): Specialist Publications.

Hoffmeyer, J. (1993). *Signs of Meaning in the Universe*. Bloomington: Indiana University Press.

Ichikawa Hiroshi (1979). *Seishin toshite no shintai* (The Body as the Spirit) Tokyo: Keiso shobo.

James, W. (1912). *Essays in Radical Empiricism*. London: Longmans.

Kaplan, H. (1980). History of psychosomatic medicine. In: Kaplan, H.I., Freedman, A.M., and Sadock, B.J. (Eds.), *Comprehensive Textbook of Psychiatry* (pp. 1843–53). Baltimore: Williams & Wilkins Company.

Kockelmans, J.J. (1999). Phenomenology. In: R. Audi (Ed.), *The Cambridge Dictionary of Philosophy* (p. 665), 2nd Ed. Cambridge: Cambridge University Press.

Kovecses, Z. (2003). *Metaphor and Emotion. Language, Culture, and Body in Human Feeling*. Cambridge: Cambridge University Press.

Kovecses, Z. (2004). Personal communication.

Lakoff, G., & Johnson, M. (1999). *Philosophy in the Flesh: The Embodied Mind and its Challenge to Western Thought*. New York: Basic Books.

Leder, D. (1992). A Tale of Two Bodies: The Cartesian Corpse and the Lived Body. In: D. Leder (Ed.), *The Body in Medical Thought and Practice*. London: Kluwer Academic Publishers.

Loy, D. (1988). *Nonduality: A Study in Comparative Philosophy*. New Haven: Yale University Press, p. 3.

Lukacs, J. (2002). *At the End of an Age*. Yale University Press, New Haven and London.

Matthis, I. (2000). Sketch for a metapsychology of affect. *The International Journal of Psychoanalysis*, *81*: 215–228.

McDougall, J. (1989). *Theatres of the Body*. London: Free Association Books.

McGinn, C. (1991). *The Problem of Consciousness; Essays Towards a Resolution*. Oxford: Basil Blackwell, 1991.

Merleau-Ponty, M. (1968). *The Visible and the Invisible*. Evanston: Northwestern University Press.

Monk, R. (1996). *Bertrand Russell. The Spirit of Solitude* London: Jonathan Cape, p. 291.

Nagel,T. (1974). What is it like to be a bat? *Philosophical Review*, 4: 435–50.

O'Regan, B., & Hirshberg, C., 1993. *Spontaneous Remission. An Annotated Bibliography*. Sausalito, CA: Institute of Noetic Sciences.

Rossi, L. (2004). Stress-induced alternative gene-splicing in mind-body medicine. *Advances in Mind-Body Medicine 2004, 20*: 12–19.

Russell, M., Dark, K., Cummins, R.W., Ellman, G., Callaway, E., & Peeke, H.V., (1984). Learned histamine release. *Science. 225*: 733–4.

Schacht, L. (Ed.) (1977). *The Meaning of Illness. Selected Psychoanalytic Writings by George Groddeck.* London: The Hogarth Press and the Institute of Psychoanalysis.

Schore, A. (1994). *Affect Regulation and the Origin of the Self.* Hove: Lawrence Erlbaum.

Shigenori, N. (1992). *Attunement Through the Body.* Albany: State University of New York Press.

Sokolowski, R. (1999). Husserl, Edmund. In: R. Audi (Ed.), *The Cambridge Dictionary of Philosophy* (p. 406), 2nd Ed. Cambridge: Cambridge University Press.

Shalom, A. (1985). *The Body/Mind Conceptual Framework and the Problem of Personal Identity.* Atlantic Highlands: Humanities Press International.

Sherbourne, D.W. (1999). Whitehead, Alfred North. In: R.Audi (Ed.), *The Cambridge Dictionary of Philosophy,* 2nd Ed. Cambridge: Cambridge University Press.

Taylor, G., Bagby, R.M., & Parker, J.D.A. (1997). *Disorders of Affect Regulation. Alexithymia in Medical and Psychiatric Illness.* Cambridge: Cambridge University Press.

Van der Kolk, B. (1994). The body keeps the score. Memory and the evolving psychobiology of post-traumatic stress. *Harvard Review of Psychiatry, 1*: 253–265.

Whitehead, A.N. (1938). *Modes of Thought.* New York: The Free Press, 1966.

Wilber, K. (Ed.) (1985). *The Holographic Paradigm and Other Paradoxes. Exploring the Leading Edge of Science.* Boston and London: Shambhala.

Wilber, K. (1998). *The Marriage of Sense and Soul.* New York: Broadway Books.

Wittstein, I.S., Thiemann, D.R., Lima, J.A.C., Baughmann, K.L., Schulman, S.P., Gerstenblith, G., Wu, K.C., Rade, J.J., Bivalacqua, T.J., & Chapion, H.C. (2005). Neurohumoral features of myocardial stunning due to emotional stress. *New England Journal of Medicine, 352*: 539–48.

Yuasa, Y. (1986). *Ki Shugyo Shintai.* Tokyo: Hirakawa shuppan.

INDEX

209